BIRTH & RELATIONSHIPS

HOW YOUR BIRTH AFFECTS YOUR RELATIONSHIPS

Also by Sondra Ray:

> *I Deserve Love*
> *Rebirthing in the New Age*
> (with Leonard Orr)
> *The Only Diet There Is*
> *Loving Relationships*
> *Celebration of Breath*
> *Drinking the Divine*
> *Ideal Birth*

Also by Bob Mandel:

> *Open Heart Therapy*
> *Two Hearts Are Better Than One*

BIRTH &
RELATIONSHIPS

HOW YOUR BIRTH
AFFECTS YOUR RELATIONSHIPS

SONDRA RAY

BOB MANDEL

CELESTIAL ARTS
BERKELEY, CALIFORNIA

NOTE TO THE READER: When we discuss a certain type of birth pattern in this book, please remember that we are describing "general tendencies" only. We are not automatically assuming that this tendency is *always* true in every single case. We know there are exceptions. For example, breech births often have a fear of hurting people in later life. This may not be true in *every case*. This is why we need help with further research and statistics.

Another complicating factor in writing this book is the fact that many types of birth overlap. For example, when trying to get research on "induced births," the individual under study may have experienced many other birth patterns along with that one; they may have been induced, drugged, breech, *and* cesarian all together! To separate out and analyze all the variables also requires more sophisticated research.

Celestial Arts
P.O. Box 7327
Berkeley, California 94707

Cover design by Ken Scott
Interior Design by Paul Reed
Typography by HMS Typography, Inc.

Library of Congress Cataloging-in-Publication Data

Ray, Sondra.
    Birth & relationships.

    1. Childbirth—Miscellanea.   2. Interpersonal relations—
Miscellanea.   I. Mandel, Robert Steven, 1943-
II. Title.   III. Title: Birth and relationships.
RG652.R39   1987   158'.2   86-28404
ISBN 0-89087-486-7

Manufactured in the United States of America
First Printing, 1987
1 2 3 4 5   91 90 89 88 87

ACKNOWLEDGEMENTS

I'd like to acknowledge the medical profession for becoming more and more open to new age birth practices and rebirthing. When I was a nurse, there was more resistance to change. One of the reasons I feel change takes so much time—even when it is so obvious change would benefit the world—is because change has fear associated with it. Just for starters, take your "first change," which was quite dramatic—from a liquid environment of the womb to the atmosphere. This was something like taking a fish from water, hurling it on the shore, and expecting it to breathe. Dr. LeBoyer says birth is like landing on the moon without any preparation. This big *change* was accompanied with a lot of pain and followed by even more (a spanking upside down), so the baby gets the thought: "Change hurts—change is very painful." We therefore get stuck at levels we should have already moved past, because we are paralyzed with the fear of getting hurt. This change from the womb is also related to *separation*—a separation from the mother's body. Therefore, change not only becomes associated with pain, but also with separation.

No wonder we resist change. This may be why we resist letting go of our ego (change) and why we take so long to heal ourselves of unwanted conditions (change). Resistance to change produces unreasonable stress—the medically-acknowledged source of a wide variety of illnesses. In order to heal ourselves, we must change. In order to have world peace, we must change. We must all adopt new thinking and entertain the affirmations that (1) change is fun; (2) change is pleasurable and easy; (3) change is natural, a scientifically proven fact of all manifest form (change is the bottom line); (4) change brings more good to everyone; and (5) change leads to unity. We must always be willing to change for the better, and to undo all wrong thinking that we may have that holds back progress for the world and ourselves.

I salute all of those professionals who are committed to the spiritual path of excellence in their work-life.

Love and gratitude,
Sondra Ray

TABLE OF CONTENTS

FOREWORD:
A DEFINITION OF REBIRTHING

The information in this book has been gathered from people exploring and reevaluating their lives through the technique of rebirthing. While rebirthing has been well described in the other books of Sondra Ray and Bob Mandel, it seems that a brief and up-to-date commentary on the technique and philosophy should be included here.

Rebirthing's predominant characteristic is simplicity. When you cease all non-essential momentary actions, the elements of rebirthing are what remain. An old Arab saying suggests that, "It is better to walk than to run; better to stand still than to walk; better to sit than to stand; better to lie down than to sit." Rebirthing can be done while walking or sitting, but the simplest and deepest way is to lie down. The body is then cared for by gravity. Breathing remains as the only required action. Rebirthing starts with lying down, relaxing, and breathing. It is to this primary life activity that we allow ourselves, finally, to give all our attention.

Long and careful attention to the relaxed breath will reveal a many-layered pattern of inhibitions and non-essential controls. These impediments to our own life-pulsation are records of earlier shocks and decisions concerning survival. The rebirthing breath systematically exposes our unconscious strategies of defense against pleasure and aliveness. When these are noticed—no longer unconscious—we can neutralize and integrate these patterns of past-time tension by breathing through them with present-time awareness of safety.

The case histories in this book are records of observations made by people who used their conscious breath as a thread to lead them out of the labyrinth of their own reactive systems. This approach is called "rebirthing" because it offers a gentle and effective way to reveal the latent pristine state of body and consciousness which we all experienced in the pre-natal time and which was progressively pushed back by the shocks of birth and early relationship. That pure consciousness is our birthright.

If this book represents your introduction to these techniques, I would recommend that you continue to explore them. Find a qualified professional rebirther and initiate the study of your own breath and the story it can reveal to you. Simple though the process is, it is both exceedingly subtle and exceedingly powerful, and we do not advise that you start by yourself. You can get the names of well-trained rebirthers by contacting the LRT International Office whose address is listed at the end of this book. Read *Celebration of Breath* by Sondra Ray for a more detailed discussion of the art and technique of rebirthing.

Our relationships can be clear and complete only when we dissolve our resistance to having that ideal condition. Unconscious birth memories bar the way as a closed portal on the path back to bliss. May the information in this book help you find the key to unlock that door.

Fredric Lehrman
Seattle, 1987

I

INTRODUCTIONS

Chapter 1

INTRODUCING SONDRA

DEAR READER,

While reading this book, you may have a tendency to skip over types of births that are not like your own and only pay clear attention to the type of birth you had. We remind you, however, that you may be living with a person who has another type of birth you should know about. What about the type of birth of your spouse, your children, your boss, your colleagues? Your relationship with these people may suddenly start to make sense after studying their births; so we hope you will pay attention to all the different types. If you are a rebirther or rebirthee, we hope this will contribute to the quality of your work or your sessions; and we encourage you to send us further research. If you are a potential researcher in this or related areas, we would appreciate your help. We admit our research is only a beginning. This book came from our experiences as rebirthers and surveys we have done. We freely admit that our statements may not be true in *every* case . . . but this is our experience in a majority of cases.

We were shocked to discover that doing surveys on birth and relationships was quite difficult, because many people "went unconscious" or became foggy and did not follow directions well. It was almost like they became "drugged." What we saw and learned during actual rebirthings seemed much more reliable.

We would like to see much more professional research done. We offer this book to "whet the appetite" on a very interesting and potentially far-reaching subject.

Some readers could criticize this book because it contains no research statistics. As rebirthers, we are not trained to do that kind of research, but we do welcome it. That was not our intention here, though it is our intention to attract those who would be interested in doing that sort of professional and scientific research.

For us, just to write this book was quite an accomplishment, because we found it to be exceptionally "activating" and "difficult to deliver." We often got "stuck" in our own birth scripts and felt the discomfort of the birth canal while trying to finish it.

For me, Sondra, this was one of the harder books I've written, and I had tremendous resistance to finishing it. I attribute this to birth being a struggle. While writing this book, I went through *six months* of sinus blockage, and I constantly remembered precise moments from my birth which have affected my relationships (see the report on my own birth). I wrote the first report on my birth at the end, just as we were finishing this book.

Needless to say, writing this book has been an experience that, once again, healed me.

It is our intention that having this information also leads to the healing of your birth and improves your relationships.

Thank you!

—*Sondra Ray*

SONDRA'S INTRODUCTION TO THE WORLD

When I was in the womb, I tried to communicate to my mother that I wanted to be born at home. Fortunately, she received this communication and honored my request. The problem, however, was that I was born on the kitchen table. Although my mother likes to tell people that "Sondra came straight from the kitchen"—as if I was some fabulous dessert—*my experience* is that it made me very neurotic about food my whole life. Whenever I would eat, or even see food, I would get nervous. All "circuits" around my birth trauma would be triggered and I would: either be unable to eat at all; would have to leave the table; would be afraid to eat my own food; or would become paranoid in one way or another on the whole subject.

I think that this affected my relationships a great deal. On the negative side, my friends were tested on patience and understanding every time they would dine with me. On the positive and more humorous side, I fell in love with several restaurateurs. I have had many unusual experiences in restaurants—from going into spontaneous rebirths, ending up with my head in my plate, to actually having very alive, romantic and exciting events happen.

My birth was apparently very "social." Relatives were dropping by, and my mother would walk around the house whistling and chatting during the labor. My life has always been very social almost to the extreme. To this day, when I hear whistling, I go into prenatal bliss.

Another problem I had was that my sister (four years older than me) wanted desperately to have a baby brother. She was so convinced that she would get one, that when I came out—and she saw I was a sister—she opened the window and said to her little friends, "We had a boy, but it came out a girl!" I immediately felt the disappointment in the room and made the decision that I was not good enough to please everyone as a female. I should have been a boy, I thought, and I have to say this affected me a great deal in future relationships. I never felt good enough as a woman, even though I was doing brilliantly and magnificently in most areas. Rebirthing healed me of this. My relationship with my sister was also not easy, right from the beginning.

A very curious situation occurred around my birth that I am sure affected my career. I had a family doctor and a midwife attend my birth. The "midwife" was my mother's best friend. She had been my dad's high school "sweetheart" and was still in love with him. She secretly wanted me to be her baby. She and my mother apparently got into a fight over what my name should be! I could pick all of this up in the womb, and at birth time, even though everyone was totally "stuffing it," I was in there, psychically saying to all of them: "Would you please tell the truth and get clear about relationships?"

I wanted my birth to be perfect and everyone in the room to be perfectly clear. I was trying to get them to change all their limiting negative thoughts by my magic powers, but I couldn't do it. So I finally just had to come out anyway. I then took a limiting negative thought about myself that went like this—"I have to sell out" and "I can't get things the way I want." I also took the thought "I can't have perfection." These three thoughts have affected me immensely all my life. I would sell out to men or women, usually men. I would give my power away. I would also set it up not to have perfection. I would always create one thing off . . . one little thing that would keep me from perfection, never quite getting things the way I wanted.

When I was born, there was a miracle. My grandfather had been in a mental institution due to severe depression over his son's death (my uncle). They released him at my birth. They say that when he first looked at me, he was instantly healed and never went back. I was not told of this and accidentally heard it from conversation between my relatives at a family reunion when I was six. Then my grandmother said "Sshh . . ." I was obviously not supposed to hear it, because it was considered weird. At the time, I made a decision that if he was healed because of me, this was weird, and, therefore, I had better not be powerful nor be the true healer that I really was. I was born a healer, but I suppressed it for years because of this. My grandfather and I had a marvelous relationship. He was always my biggest fan when I was a basketball star.

Everyone in town (population 300) knew about my birth. It was not common to have home births, so this was a big deal. Later, people would tell me that they even remembered exactly what they were doing the moment they heard about my birth. The grocery store owner's wife said, "When I heard you had arrived, I was washing my feet in the kitchen sink." All this certainly must have prepared me to be a celebrity. I have always been accustomed to having everybody know everything about me. It seems normal.

I feel very fortunate indeed that I was not separated from my mother at all for the first weeks of life. I believe this contributed to my self-esteem. I was put in a woven clothes basket, which was used for freshly washed clothes about to be ironed. I have been very compulsive about clean clothes and clothes in general my whole life. Being born a Virgo has also made me compulsive about neatness. I have always been cleaning up everything my whole life. Cleaning up places and people's minds!

*   *   *

The year that I began to "come out" as a public figure, I was shocked to recall much deeper memories of birth and many more precise thoughts. At times, I would actually walk around feeling my head being pushed out of the birth canal. Then, on my birthday, about the exact time of my birth, I experienced a sudden sinus blockage out of nowhere. I did not make the connection about my birthday until later. Everyone said I was just "burned out" from having worked in thirteen countries that year. That was partly true and all of that did push up this memory. True—but wasn't it interesting that the symptoms would get worse every day around my birth time?

Many months later, I had the privilege of teaching a rebirthing seminar with an obstetrician, Dr. Bob Doughton of Portland, who is also an excellent rebirther. In his presence, I was able to have a very precise memory of the exact placement of my obstetrician's hands on my head when I was pulled out. There was significant trauma to my right upper sinus cone below the eye. Why didn't I remember this in previous years of rebirthing? I didn't want to! It was too terrible to face.

But this particular year, I was "coming out" so much that I could not avoid it. The memory came up whether I liked it or not. Of course I could blame the doctor for being too rough and placing his hands wrong, and I could spend the rest of my life in a campaign to prevent that (which I probably will); however, I am responsible too. Probably all past-life readers would say it was Karmic, related to trauma on my face for lifetimes—which is probably true. Nevertheless, I was extremely sad about this. I had always thought I had a routine "normal" birth! I was "normal" to them, but I felt crushed.

I had tried to communicate to my delivery team just to catch me! I definitely did not want them to pull on my head at all. I was angry that they did, and I felt this in several rebirthings. I stopped after my head was out and did not want to go on. That was how my life was up until then. I was half out in the world, too. Not anywhere as far out as I needed to be. I resisted television. I was known in some groups, but I definitely was holding out on becoming a public figure, even though it was obviously my destiny. I forgave the doctor and came out a little more.

Because as a baby (who is actually a thinking being), I failed to communicate to my delivery team, I made the decision that "it is hard to get people to get how easy it could be." I was not aware of that decision either, and this created a lot of unnecessary struggle. It affected my relationship with my staff. At times I unconsciously set them up as my delivery team, and by this projection on my part, it looked like they just couldn't get it, and I got frustrated.

Another decision that came to my awareness the same year was this: "People are dying out there. . . I have to work *double*." My father's death urge had already surfaced, and I felt it at my birth—he had just been diagnosed as having rheumatic heart disease. The next thought I had was, "Oh no, I have to live with death." These last two thoughts were acted out that year in an intense fashion. I started working double. I was afraid to stop. I had to prevent death in people. I worked so hard that I nearly burned out. I did not even think of creating a vacation for myself. I could not even slow down.

I shudder to think of all the ramifications of the decision "I have to live with death." I am only now beginning to unravel the confusion that this thought has produced in my mind. Apparently, I got so mixed up around this that I ended up with something like—"If I give up death, I'll die." What was amazing to me was that I was forming all these thoughts about the exact time my sinus was getting crushed. Oh, how nice it would have been to come out onto a pillow with my mom squatting, or to come out under water. I would have loved that!

It is pretty easy to see how those decisions—"I'll get even" and "They don't see it" and "I have to work double"—have affected my relations. I wasn't giving all that I had to give to the world (people). I didn't expect people to see things easily (struggle), and I drove people nuts with my constant speeding and inability even to consider resting.

Perhaps the most influential limiting thought at my birth was this one: "I am not perfect because I am a girl—I should have been a boy to please everyone." Because of this, my life was about constantly striving to overcompensate for that thought by trying to be *perfect*! But then, I would always end up with one thing off, so I could be *imperfect*. To honor that thought, I survived, and I was "imperfect" as a girl; therefore, the way to keep surviving was to be somehow imperfect. Thereafter, perfection—which I wanted more than anything else as a Virgo—terrified me, since my aliveness was wired with imperfection.

Can you imagine the difference when I could see these thoughts and change them to "I can come out all the way now and live?" "People get what I say and it can be easy?" I can relax, and people will live, and "I am perfect as a girl."

Releasing one's birth trauma is heaven on earth. It is completely worth the time it takes to become aware of these thoughts. I assure you it is much easier to look at them than it is to keep them suppressed and have them result in pain in the body and difficulty in relationships. Facing the helplessness of not being able to get out totally on my own made me incredibly sad. I wanted just to come flying out, and have them catch me. That seemed right.

But, apparently, I got my shoulder caught when I got frustrated over the fact that everyone was not thinking thoughts that I thought they should be thinking. So I created needing to have my head pulled on. When I couldn't get out totally on my own, I was incredibly helpless. This I avoided experiencing and feeling for years. Me—the leader, always in charge, always able to do things and get things done. And yet, every so often, I would get myself into situations that made me feel helpless, and I couldn't seem to get out of them. I would have to go get help. I could not do it on my own. I wondered how I got myself into these messes. I didn't know it was my birth trauma coming up. Finally, I just had to sink into helplessness in my rebirthings. Finally, I just had to go through it.

You may wonder why anyone would want to remember all these things. For me, it was such a relief to discover answers to my behaviors that had troubled me. Seeing the truth about something tends to heal, and all I wanted was to be healed. Once I made the associations, I could let them go. Letting them go brought me liberation/freedom/joy/understanding of my relationships, and I changed for the better. I became healthier, more alive, and much happier. I woke up. I became more conscious of everything. I started getting my relationships to turn out the way I wanted. It has been totally worth it to me.

Chapter 2

INTRODUCING BOB

*I gave birth to a book today
and I feel the loss,
as though a piece of my soul
were torn from the whole
and posted for public perusal . . .*

*I can see all the people reading it,
looking for yet another new key
to an old familiar door,
answers to questions like,
"what are we here for?"*

*But for me, on the other side of the mirror,
I am exposed, a new born baby to the viewer,
and the terror of being seen
grips me like an obstetrician . . .*

*I am the mother and the child,
divided in the act of delivery;
yes, I am ambivalent knowing
this part of me has a destiny
of its own to fulfill;
cords must be cut,
and I might bleed a little
before I surrender to God's will.*

—Bob Mandel

INTRODUCTION TRAUMA

We all have "introduction trauma." When we meet someone new, we are nervous. Will they like us? Will we make a good impression? Will we like them? When we introduce ourselves to a group of people, this nervousness is intensified. We have a fear of being embarrassed, making a fool of ourselves, being criticized, or ridiculed.

Actors call this feeling "stage fright." We normal folk might describe the feelings as: not wanting to be seen; wanting to run and hide; fear of disapproval; even fear of being liked; fear of overwhelm; fear of disappearing; the desire to disappear; fear of fear . . .

The way we present ourselves to the world is governed by our first presentation to life. The first time we hit the bright lights, and people cheered our arrival, was at birth, and the ambivalence we feel towards introducing ourselves to new people and experiences is influenced by the subconscious memory of our births.

Yet life's most wonderful surprises result from new beginnings. How can we find new friends, new love, and new happiness if we cling to the old for fear that the introduction of something or someone new in our lives will turn our whole world topsy-turvy? We need the courage to take chances, to risk the unknown, and to dive into new experiences—if we are to discover wonderful surprises.

We must learn to let go if we are to touch the sublime.

This book may raise more questions than it answers. That's fine. Our purpose here is, in fact, to inspire further research, both in the individual seeking greater self-understanding and in the research community seeking greater understanding of life.

BOB'S PREFACE

What makes a person a person?
What makes a being a Personality?

Is it genetics? Are we who we are due to the limits of what we inherit—is there a scientific formula we will eventually discover that will explain what makes us who we are?

Or is it conditioning? Is our behavior in life a direct reflection of what we learn from our parents, siblings, teachers, and peers? Are we who we are because of whom we imitate and learn from?

Or is it more metaphysical than physical? Is the way we relate in life dependent totally on the quality of our (largely unconscious) thoughts, which attract corresponding experiences to confirm our secret desires? Do we have a hidden scenario, a self-fulfilling prophecy we project onto life? Is it past lives? Karma? Spiritual genetics?

If our thoughts are creative, as they seem to be, and we are the thinkers, as we seem to be, it stands to reason that our first thoughts about ourselves and relationships would serve as a context for all our future choices in relationships. The conclusions we make at birth become the unconscious legacy of our lives. The insanity of how we come into this life dictates the peculiar notion of sanity we look for in our relationships.

Such is the premise of this book!

We have interviewed hundreds of people in compiling this book, people who have been rebirthed to the point of *seeing* their births, and the decisions they made, and how these decisions have influenced their relationships in later life.

We are deeply grateful to all those who have researched their own origins in collaboration with us.

In writing this book, it is our intention to make you, the reader, more aware of the context you have chosen in which to experience love in your life. This context is fixed to the extent that you hold onto it. It can, however, be transformed once you connect with the fact that you chose it at birth because it seemed logical at the time. And the logic was circumstantial, and the circumstances have changed.

For example, your father was in the army when you were born. You concluded, "Men aren't here for me." You grow up and attract a series of men who are traveling salesmen, workaholics, live far away, or have other commitments out of town. They just aren't there for you.

Your mother was in pain at your birth, so you concluded "my aliveness hurts women." As an adult, you experience women being hurt whenever you express your aliveness, or else you withhold your aliveness to protect the women you love, then resent them for holding you back. Life imitates birth!

Your obstetrician, a kind, loving man, manipulates you at birth—in his effort to support you, he hurts you. You conclude that support equals control and pain, and, consequently, you mistrust all forms of support in your adult relationships. Your reactive stance in life is, "I'd rather do it all myself."

The body remembers (even when the mind forgets) the impressions of birth, because those memories are recorded in your cellular memory bank. We are literally in shock at birth, and our relationships in later life tend to become shock absorbers. Becoming aware of the initial choices we made—as well as the suspicion still lodged in our physical fabric—can go a long way towards the release of the primal anxiety we bring to our love lives.

We are free to the extent that we feel safe to explore change. Since birth was the first major change, any lingering, unconscious fears we have from birth affects how safe we feel with any change: change of jobs; moving to a new home; leaving a relationship; and so forth.

We can experience more love and aliveness in our relationships to the extent that we feel safe to surrender to life's energy—an energy we first learned to fear at birth. Letting go of our primal inhibitions opens us up to a world of increased joy, creativity, innocence, and spirituality.

Thousands of people have now looked at their births and the shadows they have blanketed their lives with. They have awakened and removed the blankets. They live in sunlight . . . in safety . . . in love.

You can rebirth your relationships, too. May this book be the midwife of your ideal loving relationships!

BOB'S INTRODUCTION TO THE WORLD

When I was born, I didn't have many relationships. So the first few I formed—with my mother, father, obstetrician, and nurses—were instrumental in defining my basic patterns of relating as an adult.

It was a cold, blustery December day when I came into the world. My parents had considered naming me "Blizzard," which might account for many stormy relationships later in life. It also might explain my obsession with the weather when I was in high school. I was planning to be a meteorologist at the time, and I completed a four-year project of tracking all the major hurricanes of the world. My mother always reminded me that my father forgot her coat when he came to take us home from the hospital, and that we all had to wait in the cold for a cab, only a blanket between me and the arctic air mass.

My birth itself was what you'd call "normal," which is to say your average avalanche of emotions, sensations, and impressions. It was wartime when I was born, so there was a scarcity of nurses. I was born at a Jewish hospital, but Father Divine nurses assisted at my delivery. This might explain some of my religious confusion later in life, and my unending quest for my personal divinity. Imagine being delivered by an Italian Catholic named Dr. Bruno at Israel Zion Hospital with the assistance of these funny looking nurses in habits. I remember when I told my mother I was getting rebirthed, she asked why. I said I wanted to find my divinity, and she started calling me her "divine nut"—which is perhaps an apt description of any spiritual seeker. (Getting my divinity out of its shell is often a tough nut to crack!)

My birth was quick and easy. We got to the hospital about 8 a.m. and I was born by 9 a.m. I was not a trouble-maker. The only problem was that as soon as I came out, they took me away from my mom, and she couldn't get a bed for hours. The hospital was overcrowded, so my mom was left waiting interminably until a bed opened up for her. Needless to say, she grew very frustrated. I think I got the idea very early in life that it didn't pay to be quick. I always seemed to be naturally fast, but that caused the women I loved discomfort and then I'd end up waiting for women once I was ready to go. Part of my lesson in life has been to slow down.

My mom and I spent a week in the hospital, during which time we bonded lovingly. She breastfed me and played with me, and I'd sleep in the nursery and in her bed. I sense that this week gave me a good balance of love and independence, which I've always carried with me.

I was the second born, but the first son. I guess my mom was fairly frightened, and so they anesthetized her, which is probably part of the reason my mother and my memory of the incident was so foggy for so long. It probably also explains why I became a member of the drug generation. I think there is a direct correlation between the increase in anesthesia at birth during World War II and the emergence of the druggies in the sixties. It was clear from my birth that pain killers were a necessity of life.

When I came out, the obstetrician—in all his benign ignorance—cut the cord quickly, flipped me over, gave me a good whack to get me going, and took me away from my groggy mother into the nursery. This affected my future relationships enormously, insofar as the fear of re-living this initial separation from my mother—who was the source of love and nourishment for those precious nine months—governed much of my unconscious behavior towards women. At the same time, my desire to heal myself caused me to set up situations where I was abandoned by women I loved, gradually learning (through two divorces) that I did not need women in order to survive.

My father was working at the Brooklyn Navy Yard when I was born. Being Jewish, there was a great deal of fear in my family regarding World War II. I know I was wanted as a male, but I also know that my parents never wanted me to be a soldier or fight in a war. I think being a war baby contributed to my passion for peace during the Vietnam era. I became a leading activist in the draft resistance movement and even spent a couple of nights in prison for my protests. I dodged the draft, left the country and searched for a peace outside myself. After the war, when I came home, I had realized that the only lasting peace is inner peace, and my political quest turned spiritual.

My sister, six years old, developed a serious case of hives on her eyes when I was born (she probably didn't want to see me). This compounded the guilt I already felt for hurting my mother, and throughout my relationships, my fear of causing women pain has caused me to withhold my aliveness in order to protect the woman I loved. Often, when my aliveness did express itself, it was explosive and did seem to cause women pain. Until I unravelled the source of this syndrome ("Infant Guilt Syndrome"), I felt hopelessly trapped in its jaws.

As an infant, I was fed on a schedule, every four hours, as the doctor ordered. I resented this terribly, but my vocabulary and body were too little to get me what I wanted. So I would cry and scream and be hungry and angry until the four hours were up. Then when I was fed, I would reject the food completely, spitting it out to get even with the whole damn schedule. Later in life, I rejected my mother's cooking, even throwing away the sandwiches she made me for lunch on school days.

In future relationships, meal time became crisis time, and one never knew how Bob would receive his nourishment. This also affected my money situation. I had the idea that "I can never get what I want when I want it." It seemed that my receiving was totally dependent on other people's convenience, desires, and schedules. I created umbilical attachments to jobs where the paycheck was my umbilical cord, and I'd do anything to keep it from being cut. When I became self-employed, I had to face all my fears of being the source of money in my life. The affirmation, "I can get what I want when I want it," transformed my whole cash flow and my feelings about money.

When I became a rebirther and began unravelling the effects of birth on my own relationships, I also became fascinated with how my clients' different types of delivery were influencing their relationships. It became clear to me, for example, that a premature birthee and an induced birthee would react differently in the same situation. Even more obvious was how a wanted child would be desirable in relationships, while an unwanted child would tend to attract rejection. I saw how breech births went at relationships backwards, how caesarians wouldn't complete the past, how incubator babies grew up with a glass wall separating them from love. I came to see how we re-create our births—and, indeed, the entire birth/death cycle—in our relationships, how it sticks in our minds and therefore keeps getting projected on our lives, until we locate and release the source of our scenarios—namely, our births.

In writing this book with Sondra, we have let many of our clients do the speaking for themselves. Much of the material in this book is research, research that normal, healthy human beings have done on themselves in order to generate greater happiness in their lives. It may seem to the reader that it is virtually impossible to remember things that happened so long ago, but this is not true. There are many thousands of people who have successfully unravelled the effects of their births on their relationships, and who are now living a fuller, more integrated love life as a result.

It is my prayer for you, the reader, that you may be inspired to do the same.

—Bob Mandel

II

PRENATAL ORIGINS

Chapter 3

CONCEPTION

It is said that we are conceived in the image of God. Our conception, however, is not always so divine.

Now, you may think it stretches your imagination enough to consider the ramifications of birth on life, but conception . . . ? Yet the research speaks for itself. We have had far too many cases where clients with traumatic conceptions re-created the circumstances of their origin in the conception of their relationships.

Recently, we had a student in Boston who was conceived while his mother was a prostitute. He somehow blamed himself for his mother's "evil" ways and felt he was bad. The way he acted this out was by falling in love with prostitutes, then being unable to make love with them because they reminded him of his mother. He was a victim of the "madonna/prostitute" syndrome to its ironic extreme. Like Oedipus, he was unconsciously drawn to the circumstances of his origin.

We've seen women conceived in rape grow up to be "victims" of sexual abuse, and women whose fathers died in the war shortly after their conception create lovers who mysteriously die shortly after the relationship has begun. We once had a client who was conceived the day the stock market crashed. His father lost everything. He had a pattern of creating a relationship, then going broke. We knew another man who was conceived on his parents' honeymoon, after which they stopped having sex. He had been married four times, only to have each marriage take a sudden nose dive during the honeymoon.

Illegitimate conceptions can lead to sneaky relationships. Unplanned conceptions can lead to unplanned relationships, which can
appear to lead you off purpose in your life.

The point is that the circumstances surrounding your conception
become the foundation of a great deal of unconscious patterns in
your life. Every relationship goes through a life cycle that reflects
the dovetailing patterns of the participants—conception, pre-natal,
post-natal, infancy, childhood, adolescence. The stages of growth
are recapitulated in the growth of every loving relationship.

If your origin is somehow unknown to you—stuck at some twist
in your conception—then all your relationships tend to be miscon-
ceived. If your thought at conception was negative, such as, "I am
separate from God," "I don't belong," "I'm a mistake," "I don't want
to be here," or "I cause separation" (a common thought resulting
from coming between mom and dad, intruding on their intimacy—
which later in life can lead to "incestuous triangles"), then the conception of each of your relationships will be secretly doomed from
the start. Your thoughts, after all, create results! And it won't take
long before your subconscious mind rams into your "ship of love,"
a veritable iceberg crashing into the *Titanic!*

To clear your mind of the consciousness factors surrounding your
conception, you might want to do the following creative visualiza-
tion process:

"CONCEPTION VISUALIZATION"

*Put on some calm, meditative music, and lie down with a pad and
pencil by your side. Close your eyes. Relax. Do some connected
breathing. Let yourself relax deeply, mentally, physically, and emotionally.*

Now visualize the following:

*See yourself as a disembodied spirit, a divine being of light and love
floating through the universe. (Don't try to "remember"—your in-
tellect will block you; just make it up, using the special effects of
your Steven Spielberg-produced imagination!)*

There you are, a free spirit in space-and-timelessness. Breathe!

*It is now time for you to choose a new physical form. It is the time
of your conception. You search the whole wide universe for the ideal
circumstances for this lifetime, the perfect people, places, and things
to surround yourself with—so that you may live the "good life," learn*

*what you came here to learn, teach what you came here to share. . .
You search everywhere and you choose the planet of your birth,
presumably Earth. . . why Earth?
The reason I chose to come to Earth was. . . Write down the first
thought that crosses your mind!
See yourself choosing the precise location. . .
What country? Why?
What town? Why?
What race? Why?
What religion? Why?
What mother? Why?
What father? Why?
Get clear on the last two. The reason I chose my mother was. . .
The reason I chose my father was. . .
Write down the thoughts that cross your mind.
What siblings? Why?
What economic situation? Why?
What about grandparents? Was there any illness in the family?
What about the world? Was there war? Peace? Depression?
Now it is the precise moment of your conception. You have selected
all the right circumstances. See yourself ready to embody, to beam
down. . .
See your parents making love.
What is your father thinking?
What is your mother thinking?
What are you thinking as your consciousness enters your mother's
womb?
Breathe deeply. Complete the following statements. "The reason I
chose to be alive is. . ."
"My purpose in this life is. . ."*

Most people stumble into relationships unconsciously, then wake
up from their stupor and wonder what in God's name got them
into such a mess. Becoming aware of the circumstances and conclusions of your own conception can assist you in conceiving of all your .
relationships—personal and business—in a more conscientious
manner.

If your blueprint for love (or business) is flawed, even its perfect
realization is doomed to failure. Your dream come true might be a
nightmare in disguise.

Get clear on your blueprint. Make a "shopping list" of those qualities you most want in your ideal loving relationship and begin to affirm: "I now attract my ideal loving relationship," knowing full well what you mean. We suggest reading *Two Hearts Are Better Than One*, by Bob Mandel.

Learn to say "no" to what you don't want, even when it seems to pull you head over heels into dreamland. Wake up! Love is not blind. It sees what's so and chooses appropriately. It learns its lessons well. It goes for what it really wants and is hip to the temptations that would distract it from its true purpose.

Releasing any negativity around your conception will empower you to create conscious relationships rather than chance encounters.

Seeing the perfection of your choice to be here in the first place opens the gate to choosing fully in all your relationships. Commitment is no longer a trap but, rather, a choice to follow your heart 100%.

Make no mistake about it. You were conceived in light, and your relationships deserve that same radiance.

AFFIRMATIONS FOR CONCEPTION:

    (1) I choose to be here.
    (2) I belong where I am.
    (3) I am part of God's plan.
    (4) My love is a uniting force.
    (5) My body is a safe and pleasurable place to be.
    (6) God is with me here and now.
    (7) I am chosen.
    (8) I have a purpose.
    (9) I am excited about being here.
    (10) All my choices are divinely inspired.
    (11) I conceived of a great life, and the best is yet to come.
    (12) I forgive my parents for all their fears of having me.
    (13) Thank God my parents had me.

Chapter 4

PRENATAL INFLUENCE

The time the unborn child spends in the womb is, as Dr. Verny has shown us, the busiest as well as the laziest days of our lives.

On the one hand, we can relax on a sea of supportive fluid, all our needs provided by our umbilical connection to Mother. We are in the ultimate support system available to man. Mission Control does all the work. We are back in Eden.

In later life we often seem to re-create the bliss of the womb, be it in bed with the covers pulled over us, in the bathtub, the hot tub, swimming, sailing, or just listening to the stereo, watching a movie, or driving a car—all of which are, in part, attempts to re-capture that sense of self-enclosed ease, security, support, and nourishment of the halcyon days of the womb.

And, in our relationships, we often project the desire for the womb onto our partners, expecting them to provide that sense of infinite well-being we enjoyed in Mother's belly. Some of us think that love is precisely this feeling. This kind of umbilical attachment creates inevitable separation, however, just as surely as the cord had to be cut at birth. To the extent that you feel you need your partner in order to survive, you will subconsciously push him away, proving to yourself that you are self-sufficient after all. You always have a love/hate relationship when love is based on need. Werner Erhard says, "The only reason we need someone is to have someone to blame."

The compulsion to create womby relationships leads to what *A Course in Miracles* calls "the tyranny of special relationships," where you place your partner on a pedestal above your fellow men and women. We recently saw a greeting card which expressed this type of relationship best. On the front cover it said, "It's you and me, babe, against the world." It said inside, "When do we attack?" The purpose of a relationship is not to protect us from the storms of life; love is not a fortress!

The best way through the umbilical stage of a relationship is to tell the truth and remember the Truth. Maybe the reason we blame, judge, and criticize our partners is because we're afraid to tell them we need them. So we push them away with psychic attacks. Confess your feelings of neediness and dependency. Allow your Divine Inner Child to have his say. Don't cast him away like an unwanted intruder. We all have helpless parts of us crying out for love, reassurance, and comfort. Don't be embarrassed by these feelings. They are signs of a growing strength, not weakness, a wholeness taking root at your core.

Take "helpless days" during these times. Allow your partner or a friend, to serve you for 24 hours, no obligation permitted. One day like this will save you ten sick days, which is the covert way of playing weak and helpless, while being in control.

Suppressed helplessness leads to struggle and sickness. If you suppress your neediness rather than get your needs attended to, you will grow old, senile, and dependent on others completely. What you resist can persist!

On the other hand, remember the ultimate Truth, which is that you are not helpless, you do know how to live, you can make it—indeed, you have always been a powerful survivor.

Mastering the contradictory aspects of helplessness, the truth of the feelings and the truth of the Truth, enables you to create loving relationships in which both partners are self-sufficient but choose to be mutually inter-dependent because it makes their lives easier and more fun.

*   *   *

The womb is also a busy time when the unborn child is growing rapidly—mentally as well as physically—receiving information through Mother's neurological system, as well as telepathically, interpreting feelings and reacting to their meaning.

If you were unwanted, unplanned, an accident, illegitimate, or "the wrong sex," your nine months of hiding might have seemed like 100 years of solitude, knowing that you were doomed to be a disappointment to those you loved.

If anything unusual—good or bad—happened in your family, or indeed in the world, while you were preparing yourself for this life, you probably absorbed the information on some level. If your mother sang to you, the song she sang may still be in your heart. And you may have grown familiar with the sound of her voice, as well as her thoughts, when she talked to or thought about you. In a very real sense, her thoughts were your thoughts, causing responses in your highly sensitized, unguarded little body.

You took in a lot very quickly. Imagine being in hibernation for nine months on a spaceship, a Mother Computer feeding you data non-stop while your body grows and grows and grows. The container in which you rest seems to be shrinking as your body grows. Suddenly, a red neon sign lights up, "NO EXIT TERROR!" And you start looking for a way out, groping, creeping, crawling through the dark until you finally can see the light at the end of the tunnel. When you come out of the womb, you fall head over heels into life. Out of the womb and into the frying pan, as it were.

No wonder we fear entrapment!
No wonder we all demand space in our relationships!
No wonder commitment is such a confront!
No wonder staying seems like a dead end!
No wonder it seems like we have to leave to grow!
No wonder we fear change, transition, the unknown, the future!
No wonder why change seems to mean loss!
No wonder relationships seem like a double bind!

From the day we are born, we all suffer from some form of separation anxiety. It will come up when you are leaving a relationship, a job, a home. . . We always seem to fear we are leaving something good for something bad. But it's not bad. It's just unknown. And in the unknown was our original liberation, as well as separation. So it goes round and round in our minds.

AFFIRMATIONS FOR PRENATAL INFLUENCE:

(1) *There's no escape from freedom.*

(2) *I can take care of myself.*

(3) *Since I can take care of myself, it's safe to let others support me.*

(4) *It's safe to share my helpless feelings.*

(5) *It's safe to be helpless.*

(6) *I can move through helplessness easily and pleasurably.*

(7) *The less I deny my helplessness, the stronger I become.*

(8) *It's safe to stay.*

(9) *It's safe to leave.*

(10) *I am commited to my own well-being.*

(11) *All change leads me to my greater well-being.*

(12) *The unknown is safe.*

(13) *The future is full of wonderful surprises.*

(14) *When I let go, I win.*

(15) *I am free inside.*

(16) *Since I am free, I no longer have to leave to feel free.*

(17) *I only depend on dependable people.*

(18) *It's safe to be close to people.*

(19) *I am a child of God, nurtured in the universal womb!*

Chapter 5

PRIMAL GUILT

You leave the womb with a one way ticket to planet Earth, do not pass go, do not collect $200!

And in the process of departing, you tend to form your basic pattern of leaving that governs your entire life. On the one hand, you hate to have to leave, sorry to say goodbye, and so forth and so on. On the other hand, you can't wait to get out of there, you hate putting it off, and wish you could just get it over with. Between the two hands, you carry both your fear of loss and primal guilt, trying to juggle the two as you move through life and relationships.

The INFANT GUILT SYNDROME describes the condition we take on at birth, when we think our aliveness hurts Mother, the source of life for nine months. As you squirm through the birth canal, your mother's fear of re-experiencing her own birth is "activated," causing her to hold on, shut down, and tense up, which, in turn, causes her fear and pain. Your only mistake was to conclude that it was your presence that caused her pain. "I always hurt the one I love," may have become a constant theme of your life. "I'm bad!" might be another. And so you separate from your own inherent goodness, as well as from God Himself, as psychological and spiritual guilt join forces to make you feel alone in a cold, cruel universe.

You grow up with the fear of being seen (i.e. as bad), causing you to hide in your relationships. You do not want others to notice how "bad" you really are, so you disguise yourself as "good girl" or "nice guy," seducing others into believing you are who you think you're not. Then you live in constant fear of being "found out," discovered for who you are, an impostor who really does not deserve love and happiness. How could you? You hurt people!

In your most intimate relationships, the delicate balance of your identity is severly threatened. Since love brings up anything unlike itself for healing, the more your partner loves you, the more you will feel threatened by that love, and, at the same time, afraid you will hurt your partner. The light of your partner's love will seek to shine on every shadow of your being. You will have a hard time hiding. You might try to shut down your joy and aliveness completely—in a subconscious effort to protect your lover from the pain you anticipate causing. You want to hide your "badness." Eventually, you will explode, blaming your partner for your withholding pattern, and maybe even leave—thus completing the cycle of your birth scenario.

In most relationships, people tend to seek the lowest common denominator of aliveness, then think their partner is boring or the relationship is dull. Boredom is the effort involved in suppressing another emotion—and most people are walking cases of emotional anesthesia: suppressed joy and aliveness!

You may actually go so far as to leave your partner, claiming you've outgrown her or him, as if a relationship were a pot and you the plant. This "outgrowth" myth is another recapitulation of the prenatal entrapment and the no exit terror you first felt at birth and have since held in your body like a time bomb. No wonder why an inordinate number of relationships end after nine months!

Rebirthing can assist you in locating and releasing this primal panic from your body, so that you are no longer reacting to love with the mentality of a confused, newborn child. You can attain that inner freedom, to be distinguished from external liberties, that no one can ever take away from you. You can see the conclusions you made at birth that no longer serve you and replace them with affirmations like:

(1) I forgive myself for thinking I caused anyone pain.
(2) My aliveness is a pleasure to experience.
(3) My love is good enough for me and everyone else.
(4) I am good.
(5) I am innocent.
(6) My presence is a delight.
(7) I have a relaxing influence on others.
(8) I forgive myself for pretending to be guilty.

(9) God is with me, no matter what!
(10) I deserve to have it all!

Chapter 6

OBSTETRICIAN SYNDROME

Several years ago, we were invited to speak at the First Annual Congress on Pre-and-Peri-natal Psychology in Toronto. Dr. Thomas Verny organized the conference, and we were delighted to attend, both to share our discoveries in the areas of rebirthing, birth and relationships, and also to hear what the other eighty therapists, psychiatrists, midwives, and obstetricians had to say. It was an amazing pool of research and resources for a science in the process of birth itself.

We met one obstetrician at the Congress who moved us as no other. He was about sixty-five years old, but very young at heart, and full of the milk of human kindness. If we could have chosen the ideal obstetrician, it would have been this man. In the course of speaking with him, he told us how he had delivered thousands of babies traditionally (i.e. as he had been instructed to do at Medical School), until, one day, one child changed both his mind and his life forever. He had delivered a little boy, a "normal" birth, and was getting ready to cut the cord as he always did, when suddenly he heard a loud "No!" He looked into the baby's eyes and realized, for the first time, that babies were conscious beings and that all his previous deliveries had been unconscious acts, insensitive and selfish. He told us how he used to pray that no baby would ever die on him, thereby ruining his career. He had reached a turning point, and "birth without violence" became his calling too.

Most obstetricians have a job to do, and they need the newborn baby's cooperation in order to do it well. From the baby's point of view, this relationship with the obstetrician is a powerful one, and in later relationships he will look to others to pull him out of a jam, lift him from the pit of despair, deliver him from his misery and/or otherwise help, save, and rescue him.

From the doctor's point of view, the baby might be just one of many, almost like another new car sprung from the assembly line. This is not to say that obstetricians are mechanical in their sensibility. Usually, they're not—they love babies, mothers, families, and are compassionate beyond necessity. But the bottom line is they have a job to do, and success in their careers is based on doing the job well.

Ideally, the obstetrician would be a grand master of initiation rites, who would orchestrate each baby's arrival as a celebration of life and renewal. In most delivery rooms, however, the attitude is more one of rescue than of renewal. It almost feels like an emergency room, where the obstetrician is there to save lives, not deliver healthy human beings and celebrate this magical, primal passage. Nowadays, with doctors elevated through TV to hero status, the obstetrician can become the "star" of the birth, while the mother and child are shoved aside to supporting roles.

Most relationships play out "the obstetrician syndrome" one way or the other. One partner is the rescuer, the other is the rescuee. Of course the roles can change in different situations. Just as the obstetrician was "invested" in your successful delivery, your partner can become your rehabilitator, teacher, therapist, and instructor, rather than just your co-equal creator of a loving relationship.

The Obstetrician Syndrome leads to "The Pygmalion Complex," where one partner is always trying to fix the other, rather than acknowledge the beauty and perfection that's already there. And relationships based on one person being the repairman and the other the damaged goods are doomed to failure. Once the repair work is complete, your repairman will be out the door. Or else, you will subconsciously create more damaged goods in order to prolong the agony of your unequal relationship.

If you're subconsciously playing the obstetrician with your partner, your greatest fear is that you are not needed. You have a need to be needed just as a doctor needs a sickness in order to feel gainfully employed. As soon as you are faced with someone who is truly your equal and doesn't need you, but just loves you—without your having to earn that love through helping, rescuing, or protecting—then all your unresolved feelings of neediness are likely to surface. And that's when the ball game gets interesting!

It is important to remember that obstetricians are experiencing their own birth scenario every time they step into the delivery room. If we teach what we need to learn, then it stands to reason that physicians are trying to heal themselves.

The obstetrician is the first person in our lives who physically supports, guides, coaches, controls, manipulates, and hurts us. If your experience of your delivery was marked by control-support-pain, you may have an issue in these areas in later relationships. A simple example is that you may resent your partner rushing you whenever it is time to leave. You may also mistrust any form of support, because, in your subconscious mind, support equals control, manipulation, obligation, and painful entanglement.

You may resent your rebirther for telling you how to breathe, especially if he seems to be "invested" in whether you do it right or wrong. This reminds you of the obstetrician needing you to breathe in order for his job to be a success.

You may secretly resent all your teachers, helpers, therapists, and gurus, because, although you look up to them, deep down inside, you are supremely suspicious of anyone you look up to or anyone who supports you.

It is important to forgive the obstetrician completely—to realize that he did the best he could, given his birth, upbringing, and education. And to remember that, in some sense, you chose your own birth, including the whole delivery team, and that you are responsible for what you created even back then when it seemed you were an innocent little victim!

And you made it! You survived your birth and therefore want to have gratitude, not resentment, for all those who assisted you in being here.

Your birth was ideal—for you!

AFFIRMATIONS FOR "OBSTETRICIAN SYNDROME"

(1) *I forgive my obstetrician completely.*
(2) *I can now control the way I receive support.*
(3) *Support is pleasurable.*
(4) *It's safe for me to surrender to support.*
(5) *I can do it my way.*
(6) *People support me in doing it my way.*
(7) *I forgive myself for all the times I didn't do it my*

way.

(8) *I know when I need help and when I don't.*

(9) *God is my constant support.*

(10) *Since I can do it myself, it's safe to let others help me.*

(11) *It's easy to get where I am going.*

(12) *I am perfect just the way I am.*

(13) *I can see that others know how to do it too.*

III

TYPES OF BIRTH AND RELATIONSHIPS

Chapter 7

NORMAL BIRTHS

The term "normal birth" is somewhat absurd, since, in a very real sense, every birth is normal and every birth is unique. So we all originate as ordinary extraordinary human beings. Nonetheless, since many of us are told we had this so-called "normal birth," the thought of being normal, as well as what normal means, becomes permanently embedded in our subconscious minds. Since our thoughts are creative, we may unconsciously be projecting this concept of normal onto all our loving relationships. After all, everyone wants to be normal. And we all gravitate to what is normal for us in relationships. If normal is struggle, pain, and guilt for you (because that's what your birth looked like), then you might be unconsciously looking for those same qualities in your relationship.

So, if you had a "normal birth," you may still want to re-evaluate your definition of "normal."

You may think it is not even necessary to mention a "normal birth," believing that since there are no complications, there is nothing to cover. That is exactly the problem. People who had "normal births" often feel like it was no big deal. Sometimes they feel like since it was nothing unusual, they aren't as "special" as others who had more dramatic births. There have been people we have rebirthed who had normal births and ended up with the following negative thoughts:

"I don't matter"
"I'm nothing special"
"My life is just routine"

"People don't really notice me"
"I am just ordinary"
"I am boring or blah. . ."

In some cases, we have even seen people feel guilty becuase they had it so easy, especially if their siblings had fairly difficult births. One man we know had just that thought: "People don't like me for having it so easy." He was always creating people judging him for having it easy.

It is very important to know that even in so-called "normal" births, there is still plenty of birth trauma that needs to be worked out. There was, of course, the transition from a liquid environment to an atmospheric environment which was a big shock. Usually the cord was cut too soon in your average birth. This caused fear, panic, choking, and the belief that the baby had to be turned upside down and spanked on the bottom to get it to breathe (since it was "coughing and choking"). Now turning the baby upside down and spanking it may seem "normal;" however, this is extremely traumatic to a new-born, and as we have now learned, unnecessary. This "normally delivered" baby is hanging there terrified it will be dropped, its spine suddenly straightened abruptly after having been curled up in the fetal position for all these months. This sudden change often results in back problems that are chronic and many other things chiropractors know about. Although this practice is being eliminated, thank goodness, how about all the adults walking around now who were born when this was still the common practice of a so-called "normal" birth?

One of the worst effects of a "normal" birth is getting hit or spanked in order to make one breathe. This results in immediate pain and fear being associated with breathing, resulting in the habit of breathing very shallowly on the inhale. (This is one of the main, original purposes of rebirthing: to heal the damage done to the breath-mechanism at birth. Most people are taking in very little air on the inhale and forcing the exhale. Because we are therefore "subventilating," the cells do not get the oxygen they need and deserve. This, in fact, is one of our theories of the cause of aging: the cells do not get enough oxygen due to subventilating and therefore whither and ultimately die.)

In rebirthing, we have seen people with very negative thoughts about breathing itself. This not only makes their rebirthing difficult. . .it makes their whole life difficult. Examples:

"It hurts if I breathe."
"Breathing is followed by pain."
"I can't breathe."
"I am going to hold my breath and get even."
And even: "If I breathe, I'll die."

We think you can see how some of these thoughts eventually lead to respiratory disorders such as asthma, bronchitis, and emphysema. When we have had clients with these conditions, we were able to help them track down the connection to birth thoughts upon learning to breathe. Although these thoughts may have been suppressed for some time, resulting in no illness, when something came along to trigger the birth trauma, the person often "flipped into" an asthma attack. For example, a person who was a forceps birth may be "fine." One day he walks down a street and sees a crane used to build a high rise. The crane subliminally reminds him of forceps, and suddenly he gets a migraine headache in the temples and doesn't know why. All circuits are triggered, and this leads to an asthma attack.

Other aspects of birth trauma in a "normal birth" are the sudden temperature drop (approximately 30°) from the warm womb to a delivery room that was very cold; bright lights that hurt babies' eyes; abrasive rubbing of the newborns' tender skin, resulting in the fear of being touched; cold scales, noise, scary instruments, masks; psychic contamination from negative thoughts of the delivery team and their birth traumas contaminating the space; the absence of the father; and so on.

So, if you are one of those so-called "normal births," don't pass over this book lightly. There are still thoughts you formed at birth that are affecting you. You are fortunate, however—you didn't have the extra trauma of complications, so be grateful. Furthermore, you could be living with someone whose birth will be mentioned in this book, and you may suddenly understand that relationship by reading on further.

In a relationship, therefore, a person who was a normal birth could feel as if they do not count, do not matter, and were nothing special to their mate. They could set up their mate to be more important.

If a person who was a normal delivery was hit at birth, he could have any number of negative thoughts about that which would affect his relationships. A female may have the thought: "Men hurt me." With that thought, she may be constantly (unconsciously) setting up her male partner to be her obstetrician! She could set him up to hurt her, then blame him and try to get back at her obstetrician by getting back at him (her mate). If a person was handled roughly in a "normal birth," he or she might have a fear of being touched, and this could lead to the affection in that relationship either being nonexistent or dwindling.

We have rebirthed people who had "normal births" but whose mothers had a great deal of shame and embarrassment about being exposed. Commonly, those people draw conclusions that often result in problems in their sex lives.

In some "normal births" we have studied, the doctors and delivery team were in an incredible hurry. Perhaps they had other deliveries to do. Often their reasons were understandable. However, the client had formed the thought "People don't care about me" or "People don't have time for me." This later affected their relationships, because they repeatedly set up their mates to seemingly "not care." Often they would plead for affection just at the wrong time, i.e. just at the time the mate *was* really busy. Then they would say, "See, he *doesn't* care about me. . .he doesn't have time for me."

And in every normal birth, there was, somewhere along the line, the formation of what we call the "Personal Law." This is discussed in Part V ("Birth and Business"), and it repeatedly affects relationships until it is finally cleared out. It is one of the most important things to be healed in rebirthing.

One of our clients wrote the following:

My birth was the basic no frills, hospital modern, with a touch of anesthesia to make it a little less interesting. It was normal and my relationships are normal. It was a struggle and my relationships are also a struggle. I like, both then and now, to be held. I was hurt during my birth, very painfully. I was hurt by my lover very deeply. I couldn't seem to get what I wanted during my birth, and it seems like I don't get what I want in my relationships.

A psychologist wrote us the following letter about the influence of his birth on his relationships:

The only thing my mother ever told me about my birth was that it was ordinary. . .average. . .normal. When I asked her if there was anything unusual, she'd say, "No, nothing, it was ordinary." All my life I have felt just ordinary. The truth is, I've had an extraordinary life—I was the best student in school, an excellent athlete, I am unusually successful in my work and I've had a fabulous marriage for twenty-five years. But whenever anyone asks me how I'm doing, more likely than not I'd respond, "Oh okay. . .about average." And that's how I've always seen myself and my relationships. Nothing special. Just normal. I tend to assume that I'm like everyone else, that everyone else thinks the way I do (since I'm normal), and I'm usually surprised to find out that people are different from me. Also, since I suspect my birth was somewhat painful, I tend to feel that pain is normal and that suffering is ordinary, and that since I must have hurt my mother at birth I owe it to all women to make up for that "original sin." So I'm a kind man, a do-gooder, who takes care of people. I'm a psychologist, a good husband and father. I don't make waves.

A student in one of our Workshops reports the following:

My birth was in a hospital. I am the third child; my parents were together. I experienced a lot of anger and rage from being held upside down, and fear of being alone, abandonment for being taken away from my mother. I am afraid of being alone, not in a one-to-one relationship. I become possessive, jealous. I want to be held a lot and told that they care about me.

People often get angry and disapprove of me. I want more relationships than I have because of fear of abandonment. Sometimes I want more freedom and feel smothered.

I sometimes hold onto a relationship, even though it doesn't give me anymore.

People think that I'm not there enough for them, they seem to want more of me. Maybe I'm overcompensating for people not being there for me after I was born. I feel a great need to be with people, have a lot of friends and to be in groups.

A graduate of one of our trainings writes,

The interesting thing about my birth is that my mother always told me that it was normal and it took forever. Putting those two thoughts together, I have always been late and thought it was totally normal to do so. I've lost several jobs for being chronically late. I was always late at school. I'm late with my tax returns. Isn't everyone? It's normal to be late for me. When people keep me waiting, I feel perfectly okay. In fact, I expect to be kept waiting because it's normal to be late. Once I was supposed to meet my boyfriend at a coffee shop to study a play we were reading in school. He was very late, two hours late. When he came, he apologized profusely. He was so guilty. The funny thing was, I didn't mind. I had been so busy studying the play I hardly noticed how late he was. Besides, I'm used to lateness. The play I was reading was, Long Day's Journey

Into Night. *It was long and slow. I liked it.*

One "normal, easy" birth describes how pleasure turns into pain,

*I felt as though I was being punished during birth, which actually was pleasura-
ble, but then when the doctor grabbed me and cut off my oxygen and then turned
me upside down, I felt that I had done something wrong in being born! So I
always felt I had to suffer to get love. I needed to re-create the feeling of being
punished. I had to experience pain during sex in order to feel pleasure. One of
my major decisions at birth was to be extroverted as a cover for all the pain
and guilt. When I was put in the nursery, I cried and cried and cried. I still
didn't get love. When I was hungry, they didn't feed me. I can never have enough.*

The following case was a tedious, hard labor of eighteen hours.
His mother was always proud to say it was natural and she suffered
tremendously.

*She has always been a sufferer and so have I! In relationships, I always overcom-
pensate and sacrifice myself to satisfy others. I always want to be loved and accepted and will go to any lengths to achieve that. I tend to want to be "star"
and take on leadership roles, but I somehow seem to stop before I can prove successful or complete. I'm just not really good enough for a lasting relationship.*

The next case is a very normal birth, wanted, easy, and fairly pleasurable. This kind of positive, normal delivery produced a fairly happy
child, but not without some interesting complications.

*I have always experienced an overwhelming feeling of being wanted and loved,
sometimes to the point of being stifled and wanting out, or separation. I seem
to question why I am loved so. When I came into the world, my first thought
was I needed to heal the deteriorating relationship between my parents, and I've
carried this pattern throughout my life, i.e., the feeling that I should and could
help others. There was money trauma at my birth, which was just before the
great crash of 1929. I've always had great guilt about money.*

Another easy birth reports,

*My relationships tend to be without drama or struggle. I felt loved and wanted
by my parents and have always had loving relationships. I was the first child
and I knew my parents had high performance expectations. Consequently, I often wonder if I'm doing good enough and if I fail, will people still love me? My
parents wanted a boy, and I often have felt limited by being a woman. We lived
in a small town and went to another small town hospital, where I was born;
I have always itched to travel.*

Another client, who felt his mother's vulnerability at the time of his birth, decided to be an easy birth to protect her.

I was afraid of being hurt and not cared for. The trip through the canal was an easy one, but then I created pain and separation and no mother's milk. I felt my mother's vulnerability so strongly that I took it upon myself to be her protector and savior. This was so strong that I turned against my father in silent agreement with her. She was afraid of intimacy with him and, as a result, controlled and dominated him. I bought into this and alienated him. I've been taking care of women all my life. In turn, they give me warmth and affection. I have never permitted myself to totally trust the motives of women, and since adolescence, I have never permitted myself to feel real intimate with men. When I have felt intimate with men, I have negated the relationship in one way or another.

This young man had an easy birth in a hospital, probably because his sister, born twelve years earlier, had a very difficult delivery at home.

My mom felt very confident that the doctor would take care of her, and all her needs would be met. I had a female doctor deliver me. Her name was Mag McKinley. I've lived on McKinley St. in Hollywood for the past fifteen years! I don't like to be restricted. I was a rather large baby—eight and a half pounds—and I still don't like to be bound up with clothes, blankets, etc. And I don't like to be bound up emotionally, and I don't like to be around people that are all bound up emotionally. For the past thirteen years, I have been a yoga teacher, teaching people to relax, and now I work with people in Reichean breathing, helping them to release emotionally.

A SUMMARY OF "NORMAL BIRTHS:"

(1) Many mothers will tell their children their births were normal when in fact, there were complications. These mothers tend to be covering up their guilt. Other mothers will call a birth "normal" simply because they don't remember due to a lot of anesthesia.
(2) The influence of your "normal" birth on your relationships will ultimately depend on what is being called "normal." Is anesthesia normal? Then drugs, pain-killers, and other addictions may seem normal to you. Is forceps being called "normal?" Then headaches may be a normal part of your life. The point here is that many so-called "normal" births are in fact, somewhat more complicated.
(3) If your birth was really normal, in the sense of easy, relatively

fast and mostly pleasurable, you may grow up to: be easy-going and like people; feel more wanted and loved; have less drama and struggle in relationships; be a relaxed person; feel close to your mother; be able to take care of yourself, handle being alone; feel comfortable with intimate relationships.

(4) On the other hand, you may: feel like there's nothing special about you; feel like one of the crowd; be an average Joe; be afraid of being different; be afraid of excelling; be a hopeless conformist; find life itself just ordinary.

AFFIRMATIONS FOR "NORMAL BIRTHS:"

(1) *I am a unique individual.*

(2) *I am an important part of God's plan.*

(3) *I make a difference.*

(4) *I have a valuable contribution to make.*

(5) *I am an extraordinary human being.*

(6) *It's safe to be a little strange and different.*

(7) *I am abnormally wonderful.*

(8) *I am unusual.*

(9) *It's safe to take risks.*

(10) *I am exciting to be with.*

(11) *I am God's gift to the world, and the world is God's gift to me.*

Chapter 8

UNWANTED, UNPLANNED, ILLEGITIMATE

Many children are unwanted, unplanned, "accidents," or illegitimate. In the final analysis, no child is truly unwanted because parents' results really reveal their true intention, i.e., what they get is what they subconsciously most desire. Still, often a child will feel unwanted, as though he or she were the last thing on his parents' mind.

Sometimes, in the heat of frustration, a parent will even scream at a child, "I wish you had never been born!" Probably, the child feels the same way himself.

An unwanted child will have a difficult time growing up to feel wanted as a mate. He will tend to have a problem in feeling his own worthiness of love, often thinking he doesn't even deserve to be alive. And if someone does come along who wants him deeply, he will play his parents' role and reject the love that is being offered. Such is the power of the loyalties of our unconscious mind.

An unplanned child may be addicted to lack of organization in his life. Not planning becomes a way of survival. Flowing with it becomes an addiction. A simple goal can become a life-threatening experience.

We recently had a sixteen-year-old boy as a student. He came to a training because his parents bribed him. His story was thus—nine months before the training he got into two automobile accidents. Now he wanted a new car. His parents said they would only allow him the car if he came to the Loving Relationships Training and took responsibility for creating the accidents. During his rebirthing, we asked him, "Do you think your birth was an accident?" He answered, "Not my birth. I was wanted. But my conception was an accident." He had the thought he had to create accidents in order to be here. We gave him the new thought, "I'm meant to be here," and his face lit up like an angel.

In the rebirthing community, we have welcomed many orphans. Their fear of rejection is often so great (and sometimes so denied) that they will do anything to win love. Usually, they are "nice guys" or "good girls" who endear themselves to you by taking care of your needs, chores, and small jobs to be done. They are born "go-fors," wanting to make you need them so they'll feel loved and wanted. In fact, they are compensating for thinking they are unwanted by making themselves indispensable. They need to be needed. And if you tell them they don't need to earn your love, they can get very confused.

If you were an "accident," then all your relationships can seem like accidents, chance encounters that happen to you. Love will be truly blind. You will have a block in seeing how you create these accidental relationships, because in your mind creation equals accidents.

If you were illegitimate, your whole life tends to go underground. In some cases, a mother is so embarrassed about an illegitimate conception that she attempts to hide her pregnancy. The child grows up thinking that he must hide to survive. Often what he will hide most is his own sexuality. Sometimes he will have a problem legitimizing his life in any sense. We know one such case where a man couldn't pay his taxes, because he was terrified that if he became legitimate, they'd find out he was illegitimate. Crazy, but true!

We know another case in which a woman wouldn't get married, because marriage was legitimate and she wasn't. This lady was the illegitimate daughter of a famous politician—she would never even tell me who it was. As a baby, her mother would bring her to a pre-arranged street corner, where the father's black limo would park so he could see his child. This lady grew up to have very sneaky relationships, and strange rendezvous in bizarre places.

One unwanted client wrote us,

I knew I was unwanted. So I delayed coming out. I was late and very big. I caused my mother pain. I felt rejected by both my parents.

I never feel ready for a relationship, yet I crave closeness. I struggle to avoid rejection, but I always feel there is something wrong with me. I want to be more intimate, but I'm afraid to be trapped if I get too involved.

Rejection is always inevitable. I'm always trying to prepare myself for the worst.

One young lady reports,

Although I don't know the physical condition of my birth, I know that they wanted a boy. I was not breastfed. My mother had a pain killer and my father did not want me because there was not enough money.

I feel those conditions manifest in my life in that I'm always alone and generally unhappy unless being entertained. I live through my men until I realize that they are little boys and that I totally dominate and manipulate them.

I reject people who love me and doubt that anyone could love me—feel that they want something from me.

I know my worth in the universe psychically but feel totally worthless inside. I long for a mate through and with whom I can grow and not outgrow. And one who accepts me for myself.

I detest children and see them only as a burden, although I know that they can bring great joy.

Another young lady reports,

My birth was unplanned. My father had to marry my mother. My father asked my mother to get an abortion. She was furious and said no.

I feel like I'm not good enough or lovable enough for an exclusive relationship. Because my father had to marry my mother, he couldn't date other women and he wanted to. So, if I have an exclusive relationship with a man, he can't see other women, and I'll be denying him what he wants. I'm an interference and an intrusion in men's lives. I do not have long-term relationships. The longest one I can think of had many gaps in between where we didn't see each other.

Another woman writes,

A way my birth affects my relationships is I wasn't wanted. How that looks is: since my father rejected the fruit of my mother's womb, I'm now not willing to allow a man to experience the warmth of mine; as for my relationships with women, they tend to be very sensitive and over-protective.

A graduate of one of our workshops writes,

Several attempts were made to abort me. My birth was natural, at home. A doctor was present. My mom nursed me.

I've always felt scared of rejection and a great need to please everyone. I have a strong need to be liked. I mistrust others' real feelings towards me. I lack confidence in approaching new situations or people. Socially, I feel unworthy.

I very strongly question people's love. How can you love me? I'm unworthy.
I usually underestimate myself or accept situations less than my true capabilities.

One client writes,

I felt that everyone was mean to me when I came out, and as it was happening, I was angry and decided this was too hard and I didn't want to do it. My father was angry and my mother was scared. They didn't want me, I felt abandoned and all alone; as if nobody cared. This affects my relationships today because I expect rejection and pain. Also there is still the feeling, "I won't do it," as a recurring theme in my life. I fear abandonment and am always angry.

One young man was unwanted and pulled out with forceps,

My mother tried to abort me, and I didn't want to come out. My mother had a bad heart, and there were a lot of people in the delivery room, all with a different opinion of what to do with her. I was afraid she would die if I were born.

In relationships, I don't feel safe. I'm always afraid they will leave, because I push them away or they will die. I always feel unwanted and unloved. I'm not worthy of being loved, because I hurt people.

One unwanted woman reports,

The way my birth affects my relationships is I don't want to be separated from those I love, so I keep every relationship frivolous and distant. If I get too close, I get serious. It's too much trouble, responsibility, and no fun. Therefore, I don't trust and resist accepting affection. I run away from it when I get it. I feel I'll lose it if I do it. I feel if I'm not good enough, they will leave. I create a relationship maintenance that is too heavy a responsibility. It weakens the Holy Relationship I have with my new self.

Another case:

I was illegitimate. I wasn't supposed to be here. The way my birth affects my relationships is that I am very nervous about getting started in a relationship; it causes a lot of upset for me. Thinking about relationships causes my stomach to be upset. I love to be in relationships, but I have learned to function very well without an intimate relationship, and now thinking about getting into one makes me nervous.

I feel unworthy, unwanted, and unlovable.

One illegitimate baby writes,

The significant facts about my birth were:
(1) My mother was not married when I was conceived: She married my father when she was three months pregnant with me; (2) my father asked my mother to get an abortion. She was furious at the suggestion; (3) I am the first of seven children; (4) the evening before my mother gave birth to me, my parents were at a wedding reception, and my father asked my mother not to stand by him because she was so pregnant he didn't want to be seen with her.

The way my birth affects my relationships is that I attract men whom I feel have everything and what can I add to their lives—nothing—so the relationships aren't lasting and I always feel insecure even at the best moments. Also, I have two children, and feel I cannot have a meaningful, lasting relationship by bringing them into it. So I have had men tell me they don't want to raise any more children, and it would make a difference if I had no children. And I feel children are a burden and get in the way of romance and loving relationships.

I feel I can not be enough, or a total person, to satisfy anyone so that they would want an exclusive relationship with me. There always seems to be another woman. Often times I attract married men, and put myself through a lot of heartache.

Another illegitimate case reports,

I was illegitimate. I was small. My father wasn't there. I didn't bond with my mother. I was born in a hospital.

How my birth has affected my relationships is mainly feeling no one wants me the way I feel I want to be wanted, and I always have a strong fear that if I'm involved with someone, they will leave me. I never feel men are really there for me, and I often feel like I need to hide my relationships from friends and family, because they're not what they should be. I also constantly feel like I'm unlovable.

Another "unwanted" writes,

I had a long, difficult labor and delivery because I was unwanted. My parents were worried about money, and my mother was scared and had to be drugged.

If I don't feel wanted in relationship, I shut down the space and stop being loving to my partner. The unwantedness can come up in sex, choosing what we do, or just spending time together. I don't like ending relationships, because I know how much it hurts.

And still another unwanted woman writes,

I was born natural on the kitchen table. It was very painful to Mom. I was not wanted. I wasn't a boy like my older brother. He was very loved. She hated sex—all males except her father and son, hated poor Dad.

I tried hard to control my relationships with men. I look for men who are weak. Yet when they give in to me, I lose interest in them. Strange men excite me, but I'm afraid of them; I'll lose myself and end up with nothing. Was married twenty-five years to a great man that I was top dog with. When he got tired of me leading him around and hassling him, he left me.

One client reports,

I had a routine hospital birth. I was my mother's third and easiest, she said. Also, unplanned. My parents were practicing rhythm, and I syncopated right in. There was a lot of fear, guilt, and confusion between my parents. In relationships, I think I have to protect myself and use distance, aloofness, coolness, to keep others from getting too close or pushing me too far or too fast.

A lady writes,

I was illegitimate. My birth was in Albuquerque, New Mexico, where my mother and grandmother were nursing their favorite son and brother who was dying of TB. I was conceived before my mother married the man I knew as my father for twenty-one years.

I was delivered by an MD and considered premature, as I weighed under 5 pounds. The man my mother married was not present when I was born. At the age of twenty-one, in anger, my mother told me about my father—that he was a short red-head, that I walked like him, that he wanted to marry my mother. The reason? That I would be a girl and she would name me Tempest, for that's what I would be all my life. I've searched for this father all of my life and just recently forgave my mother for her transgressions. I've spent my life feeling unwanted. Thanks to rebirthing, now at sixty, my life is really turned around!

SUMMARY OF UNWANTED, UNPLANNED, ILLEGITIMATE:

You will, if you are this type, tend to be:
  (1) addicted to rejection in relationships;
  (2) play the other role and reject anyone who wants you;
  (3) try to make yourself indispensable so you won't be rejected;
  (4) be sneaky if you were illegitimate;
  (5) have trouble with taxes, marriage, and other legitimate forms if you were illegitimate;

(6) have trouble planning if you were unplanned;
(7) be a compulsive planner if you are over-compensating;
(8) be accident prone if you were an "accident;"
(9) be disorganized if you were unplanned;
(10) feel like relationships take you off course if your birth seemed to come at the wrong time for your parents.

AFFIRMATIONS FOR UNWANTED CHILDREN:

(1) *I am a wanted man (woman)!*
(2) *I deserve to be alive.*
(3) *I am irresistable!*
(4) *I am God's gift to the world, and the world is God's gift to me!*
(5) *I forgive my parents for not having the self-esteem to want me.*
(6) *I choose to be wanted.*
(7) *It's safe to be wanted.*
(8) *I have the legitimate right to be loved and wanted.*
(9) *I have a purpose God would have me fill.*
(10) *I am a chosen child of God.*

Chapter 9

WRONG SEX

In many Loving Relationship Trainings, we do a survey in the birth section and ask "How many of you were not born the sex your parents wanted?" You would be amazed at the number of hands that go up! Maybe both parents got a baby of the opposite sex from what they wanted, or maybe just *one* of the parents. Either way, imagine how the baby feels! Remember always that the baby *in utero* is a *conscious*, thinking being. It already knows *in utero* if the parents want the opposite sex from what it is! Many do not want to come into this pending doom. . .they know there will be disappointment.

Some of the thoughts that these babies form are:

> "I'll NEVER be good enough as a woman (or man);"
> "I'm a disappointment;"
> "I am the wrong one;"
> "I am confused" (in the case where one parent wanted a boy, the other a girl);
> "I'll never be able to please people;"
> "I should be a boy" (decision made by a female baby if parents wanted a boy);
> "I should be a girl" (decision made by a male baby if parents wanted a girl).

In most of these cases, the situation seems hopeless, never subject to change or improvement, so the child faces doom unless it has a sex change (or changes the thoughts completely).

In a relationship, the person often feels he is never going to measure up. Let's say a female baby grows up in a family where they wanted a boy. She may become quite a tomboy in order to please them. If she does become feminine and creates a relationship with a man, she may pick one that will subtly or overtly put her down so she can feel not good enough as a woman. She will keep trying and keep failing.

Of course, the problem is that she will tend to pick a mate who will perpetuate the issue, a mate who probably has a need to put women down. This destructive game will go on and result in hurt until the partners see the truth and do something about it. This woman may also pick a career in which she can function like a man. In fact, she may subtly be constantly competing with men in many ways that are not obvious to her. She may have a lot of difficulty receiving from men. She may always be giving men a double message: "Treat me as a woman, but I really require you to treat me as a man." A woman in this situation has to learn that she can please people by being a woman.

In all cases of this type, we would ask these rebirthees to take responsibility for the fact that they chose to incarnate into a family where the family wanted something other than what they were. We would ask them why they did not want to be wanted for the sex they were. This is a part of their CONCEPTION TRAUMA, and in their soul journey, they must face their choices responsibly. The affirmation is: "I forgive myself for not wanting to be wanted as a woman and blaming others."

Of course, it is obvious that future parents should be, and often are, pleased with whatever sex they are given and understand that it is perfect for them in many ways. However, clearly it is ideal that this level of acceptance be reached *before conception* and not just at birth or during the pregnancy.

This story is mentioned in the section on finances but applies as well here. A wealthy man, who gambled at Monte Carlo, bet a lot of money that he would have a boy. He had a girl. She grew up, hearing from her father the oft-repeated statement: "You cost me a lot of money being a girl." She adopted the thought "I cause men to lose money." In her life, she had married two millionaires. They both lost almost *all* their money when they were with her!

The following is an example of a written report:

I was a face presentation, home birth, no drugs—forty-eight hours of labor. My parents wanted a boy, especially my father.

The major way my birth has affected my relationships is that I thought that I always had to do the opposite of what people expected. Since I chose to turn around and come out face up instead of face down, I have always rebelled all my life. One major way I rebelled was to choose to marry a man who was really the opposite of what my family and myself wanted for me. My family was very rich; he was definitely poor.

In my past relationships, I have been very argumentative. I would always argue and take the opposite viewpoint of my mate. If he said the sky was blue, I would find a way to disagree about the sky not really being blue and point out the clouds. No matter what, I just could not be agreeable.

The main reason I chose to turn and come out opposite was my parents wanted a boy and I decided to be a girl. I made the decision I was the opposite of what my parents wanted, so with my family, my mates or anyone I was really close to, in some ways I would do the opposite of what they wanted or I would disappoint them in some way. I would also create people who would disappoint me.

Growing up, my dad always played catch with me and took me to sporting events. Since I really loved my dad and knew, unconsciously, I was supposed to be a boy, my father was really my role model. I tried to do things that my father would be proud of and give me attention for. I was on the girls' basketball team and the swimming team. I was very athletic in high school.

All my closest friends in high school were boys, except for a few best friends. It was always easier for me to relate to boys than girls. I have had steady relationships with men, nonstop, from age sixteen to thirty-six. The majority of these relationships started out as friendships, leading later to romance. I had learned how to be a good friend and play things the boy's or man's way. In my first relationships, sex seemed a problem. I didn't quite know how to act the girl part of me. I had a lot of confusion around balancing my dominant male side with my less cultivated feminine side. This shifted with rebirthing. I started looking at myself as being a beautiful woman, and I learned how to enhance my femininity. Sex also improved in my relationships after rebirthing, because I could be a good playful friend and also a feminine sexual partner.

As I got closer to what I thought was my balance point, something very unusual happened. I found myself attracted to and attracting gay men. This gave me the opportunity to look outside of myself as a mirror of my inside confusion. I was attracting men who wanted to be with a man, because I had been confused about my own sexuality.

My confusion about my sexuality also affected my career and my life purpose. I had gotten a master's degree in psychology of early childhood. After my divorce, I ran back to Daddy and tried to be his son. I worked for him for three years learning the family business. As I became more and more involved with the Loving Relationships Training, I realized I was not really doing what I loved. I always did what my father loved, to please him. I felt if I left the business, I would lose my father's love. But when I really went for what I wanted, he supported me 100%. My father acknowledged me in an LRT training for having the guts to do what I wanted with my life, and I have felt nothing but approval from both my parents ever since.

The more I put myself out in the rebirthing community as a center manager or trainer, the more I would have reactions to my presentation not being appropriate for who I really was.

People would see me in a different light than I thought I was presenting myself. Often, I would have people disappointed in me. This would stop me from wanting to come out and really show myself as the powerful woman I knew I was. I always had a lot of nervousness and fear whenever I would talk in front of groups. My fear was that people would be disappointed in who I really was, so I had a tendency to hold back and not present my true self.

I also had a strong right/wrong issue which made me very defensive in relationships. If the people I loved gave me feedback, I would try to prove that I was all right the way I was. However, I soon learned that if I listened to what people told me, realizing it was from love and support, I would change my thinking quickly. I learned that the more I listened to people's feedback, the more people listened to me.

Since I had made the decision that I was unwanted as a woman, I always created men who did not want me completely as a woman. Or, if they wanted me as a woman, they would not give me what I wanted. Since I decided to be a girl—which I thought my parents didn't want—I felt that I didn't deserve to get what I wanted from the men I loved.

The decision I had about being unwanted as a woman also kept me from letting men want me. I never wanted the men who wanted me because this would not compute for me. I would somehow disappoint the men who wanted me, or I would chase them away. If a man would love me 100%, I would somehow find a way to be disappointed in him. Our thoughts go both ways: I would have to disappoint a man if he wanted me, because if he wanted me, something must be wrong with him.

Through rebirthing, the LRT, and the use of affirmations, I am reversing all my wrong thinking. I now realize I am a suprisingly wonderful woman who deserves to be completely wanted as a woman, by a man I want.

One young man whose birth was easy, except that his mother both wanted a girl and began a long term illness during the pregnancy, writes:

I see now why it is difficult for me to be responsible for being a man. Why I have a lot of sadness and anger. Why I'll do anything for people to love me. I see *that I resent being here because of how I was received at birth. Also, I have a hard time quitting cigarettes—my father missed my birth because he went out for a cigarette. I have the thought I'm not good enough.*

One young lady, who was late probably because her parents both wanted a boy, also mentions that her mother did not like to touch her. She also writes that,

I have problems accepting myself as a woman and try to get men to reject me. I have had a tendency to fall in love with homosexuals, and then my feeling is there is nothing I can do to please him because I can't become a man. I feel that nobody wants to touch me, that there is something wrong and terrible about me. I mistrust people. I am the most happy when I am alone. I feel that people intrude on me (exactly how I felt in the delivery room), destroying the beautiful world I live in by myself (the womb). I feel a lot of resentment towards people. I want to be independent and do things my own way.

Another woman, whose grandparents wanted a boy, concludes,

I always tried to please, never made waves or brought attention to myself. I was very athletic and competitive with the boys and always had lots of boyfriends. I was suspicious of women, because my mother tried to abort me, so I've always felt more comfortable with men. Triangles were always happening in my life. . . trying to take boyfriends away from my girlfriends. My uncomfortableness with my femaleness came up when I got my period and grew breasts. I became withdrawn, and felt drugged, and was never satisfied at the moment. I always had the thought that if this or that would happen, then I'd be okay or happy. I always fell in love and then became dissatisfied and looked elsewhere.

SUMMARY OF WRONG SEX:

People who were not the sex their parents wanted tend towards the following:
   (1) they have difficulty with their gender and/or are afraid to take responsibility for their gender;
   (2) they feel unaccepted;
   (3) they feel sad, angry, and resentful in relationships;
   (4) they cannot accept themselves in relationships;
   (5) they feel dissatisfied in life;
   (6) they don't know what is expected and don't know what to receive in relationships;

(7) more often they see the world as an unfriendly place, and the same for relationships due to sex identity problems;
(8) puberty was a big problem;
(9) sometimes they are happier alone;
(10) they fear being disappointed.

AFFIRMATIONS FOR WRONG SEX:

(1) *Thank God I'm a man (woman).*
(2) *I am a wonderful surprise.*
(3) *I am God's gift to the world.*
(4) *I forgive my parents for not knowing what they really wanted.*
(5) *I am desirable.*
(6) *I am irresistable.*
(7) *My body suits my purpose.*
(8) *I am the right one.*
(9) *My sex is right for me.*
(10) *I am highly pleasing to myself in the presence of others.*
(11) *People are pleased by my presence.*
(12) *My presence is a complete pleasure.*

Chapter 10

PREVIOUS MISCARRIAGES, ABORTIONS, OR FETAL DEATHS

Whenever we do the first interview of a new rebirthing client, we always find out if there were any miscarriages, abortions, or fetal deaths prior to the pregnancy of that person. This is important information for several reasons.

The mother was likely to be worried about the possible death of this being. This creates "prenatal trauma" and adds a lot of fear to the pregnancy and consciousness of the person who was in the womb.

The person often ends up with a lot of fear of loss, fear of death and feels in general "unsafe."

If there was an abortion prior to this baby, the mother may still be suffering from a lot of guilt, which will also affect the pregnancy and baby.

Sometimes the baby actually feels he is supposed to "replace" the former one who died. This creates added psychic pressure.

Sometimes the former being was actually the *same* soul, but did not "make it" the first time. I usually ask, "Does it seem like the baby that miscarried or died before you, might actually have been you?" Often times this question produces an immediate emotional reaction and the person *feels*, with certainty, that yes, it was actually so!

In the case of the latter, this being may therefore have the thought that "in order to live, I have to die first." Although this sounds bizarre, we have had many cases on this order. These people tend to create what we would call a lot of "mini-deaths" before they can enjoy life. They end up with the unfortunate dilemma "The more I live, the more I have to die." It is very complicated rebirthing, and it took us quite a few years to learn how to unravel the birth-death cycle of this kind of individual. We had a case in Seattle where the person, a female, related to me that her mother had had *seven* male babies, all fetal deaths, *post partum*, before she was ever conceived! These pregnancies were actually *her* trying to come in as a male. She finally gave up trying to make it as a male, which she could not seem to do for whatever Karmic pattern she had as that sex. She returned as a female and survived. During her rebirthings the memories of not making it as a male were very clear to her.

Although we are very careful not to add any guilt around the abortion issue, it is something that the rebirther and rebirthee must face if it is part of that person's karma. If there was an attempted abortion that failed, we compliment the person for having a strong life urge and help them forgive everything. By helping them take responsibility for choosing their parents, and even that incident in their "birth script," they get unstuck from the anger and blame they might have had. Some of these people do grow up with the fear that someone is out to kill them, obviously. Most often, they have the thought "I shouldn't be here." Trying to live life with that thought is difficult and no fun. In one extreme case, a man remembered (after a few years of being around us off and on) the actual memory of his mother trying to abort him with some kind of "instrument." He decided that maybe if he would "play dead," she would think it was "over" and stop poking around. This worked. She stopped poking around. He kept "playing dead" until she got over her resistance and she *finally* accepted the pregnancy. The only problem was, he adopted the thought "In order to survive, I have to 'play dead.'" This resulted in him having to pretend that he "didn't get it" (life or enlightenment). He took all the life-supporting seminars he could find but could not actualize them because he had to pretend not to be alive. We have to acknowledge this man for coming back and back until he felt safe enough to uncover this incredible "wiring." We'll never forget the day that he finally "let us in" to his mind completely after a very deep rebirth. All of us were overjoyed.

The "liberation" for these people is, once again, getting out of blame for "people trying to kill me" and forgiving oneself for "setting it up." The affirmation may be something like this: "I forgive myself for not wanting to live fully, and for blaming others." "I forgive myself for using others to end my life." "Now I choose to be totally alive and live fully." "The more I choose to live, the happier I am."

There is often a subtle "Catch-22" for people involved in this kind of thing. Because they did not want to be here fully, their lives can be miserable. Because their life is miserable, they often don't want to be here. To them, the "solution" seems like "checking out." And yet, death is no solution. It is not mastery at all. The real solution is *wanting* to be here. But since they are miserable (and feeling unwanted), it is often tricky to get them to want to be here.

They need to write the affirmation "The more I choose to be here, the happier I am, and the happier I am, the more I want to be here" over and over until they can "GROK" it. We have had very good results with this by having them write this affirmation over and over and having them mail these pages so we can make sure they are actually *doing* the affirmations.

* * *

"DEATHS IN THE FAMILY AROUND PREGNANCY"

Some clients with this in their environment came out early by choice, because they could not stand to stay in the womb, since the mother was so upset. They felt so uncomfortable that they thought they would die if they stayed in, and yet they nearly died by coming out early. In many books by the mystic schools of Tibet, we have read that it is very important to keep a mother who is pregnant away from anxious people, sick people, and dying people—and especially from funerals. It is very important that a pregnant woman is not made to feel guilty if she does not want to attend a funeral of a family member during the pregnancy. One client we rebirthed remembered a prenatal experience where a grandfather died. His mother was completely torn with the conflict of not wanting to go to the funeral because she was pregnant and feeling guilty if she didn't go. The guilt won out. She went to the funeral. It was agony for her and the fetus. Needless to say, it is important for everyone around a pregnant mother to be immersed in life-supporting situations.

Post partum: Let's say someone in the family dies right after birth. The same holds true as above. This could affect the milk and the hormones of the mother. This could affect the sex life of the couple. This could affect the bonding with the baby and on and on.

Everyone's health could break down.

If these unfortunate circumstances do or did occur, we would recommend the following:

1. A lot of rebirthing during this time.
2. Doing many aliveness enrichment affirmations.
3. Reading the immortalist literature.
4. Praying to the Masters for release from the death urge.
5. Doing anything and everything one can think of to strengthen the life urge.

Again, we say, if you feel like a victim of such a circumstance, doing the above NOW will still work to release you. It certainly would be helpful to know if any of this happened around your birth or the birth of your mate. Some of the ways this might affect relationships:

The person might think: "I can't be fully alive. I better stay depressed and sad if I am to get approval;" "I came at the wrong time. This is a bad time for me to be here;" "I don't know how to make my mother or father happy." (This could result in "I don't know how to make my mate happy.")

These thoughts will obviously affect relationships. Also, if everyone was depressed around this person's conception, pregnancy, or birth, he may tend to attract depressed types of people with dead energy into his life, especially as mates. Think about it. The mind seeks familiarity. If there was a family death before or after your birth, you may have spent a lot of time relating to *that*, and thinking that is what life is about. This can be released, but it does take awareness first.

The main point in healing this kind of trauma is to get yourself out of blame. Stop blaming yourself and stop blaming your mother. If you blame yourself, you will be stuck in guilt. Guilt demands punishment, and so you will tend to spend much of your life making things difficult, punishing yourself, using many various means. Or, if you blame your mother, you will still feel guilty for not forgiving her, so you will still probably punish yourself.

An actor told us the following:

My mother had a miscarriage. Then she got pregnant with me. She was afraid she'd lose me too. . . I've always felt like I might be the wrong one. . .maybe that I wouldn't be here if the first child hadn't been miscarried. . . . In my career as an actor, I find it hard to take parts away from other actors. . . . I'm guilty when I do get parts. I never get hired as a replacement, and I live in constant fear of being replaced myself.

A graduate of the LRT reports:

My birth was natural, but there had been an attempt to abort me at three months. I came out with the cord around my neck. My father was not there and my parents could not afford me. My sister was jealous so, to me, life was a dangerous place to be. Life was a struggle! I felt alone and I must do everything alone. I am very afraid of life, because I think people are out to kill me. Life hurts and therefore I don't want to live.

A rebirther wrote us the following:

One of my clients had an interesting experience. His mother tried to abort him three times during pregnancy. He grew up, fell in love, and got married. Every three years he and his wife had a major upheaval in their relationship. They got divorced three times, every three years, until now they've finally made it through a four-year cycle. Needless to say, his mother's attempted abortions were all at three months!

Another student reports:

My mother tried to abort me twice. When I did come out, I was breech and felt turned, twisted, and unwanted. I have a fear that women will leave me because I am not good enough. Also, I don't feel good enough for the following: a good relationship; to feel loved; that it will "turn out" the way I want it; to get the attention I want. I don't feel like I belong with powerful people so I withdraw. I don't trust people because I know they will hurt me, especially the ones I love. The bottom line is I don't feel loved. I'm unwanted!

Another LRT graduate writes:

I had an easy hospital birth, but there was a miscarriage before me. Dad wasn't there. Men seem to be gone for me most of the time in a close relationship. My relationships tend to be traumatic. . .painful. I have to work a lot to make it. Maybe the fear of miscarriage makes me work overtime. I feel like Saturday's child. I have to work for every bit of approval and acceptance. It is a continuous job to re-earn approval all the time. I have a terrible fear of not making it, falling short, failing. Do I deserve to make it when others don't?

SUMMARY OF ATTEMPTED ABORTIONS:

(1) They are more afraid of life;
(2) often think people are out to kill them;
(3) often have the thought "I don't want to live;"
(4) often have the thought "Life hurts;"
(5) they don't usually trust people in relationships;
(6) they don't feel wanted or loved in relationships;
(7) they feel like they "shouldn't be here."

SUMMARY OF PREVIOUS MISCARRIAGES:

(1) They expressed more fear;
(2) they had the tendency to be concerned about things, often in an extreme way.

AFFIRMATIONS THAT MIGHT HELP ARE:

(1) *The more I live the more alive I am. The more alive I am, the more I live.*
(2) *I can survive without being dead. . .I can survive being alive.*
(3) *Life is safe, living is safe. The more alive I am the safer I am.*
(4) *I can start living right away and keep on living.*
(5) *I can let go of death and survive.*
(6) *I am safe and immortal right now.*
(7) *There is nothing to fear. I am alive.*
(8) *The more I give up worrying the more alive I am. Life is what I want.*
(9) *I am responsible for my own joy and pain and others are responsible for their own joy and pain.*
(10) *People are happy that I am here.*
(11) *I bring joy and fun to people naturally.*
(12) *I make things easier and better for people.*
(13) *People always get better in my presence.*
(14) *People are glad that I am alive and they feel more alive in my presence.*
(15) *I forgive everyone and everything at my birth and after my birth that was unpleasant.*

Chapter 11

FAST OR HELD BACK

Sometimes when people have a "fast" birth, others have a problem with it. It has been our experience with clients like this who "remember" their birth that for them, it was not a problem. However, others around the birth thought it was not "normal" and therefore dangerous.

Some of the thoughts the baby might adopt are: "I'm wrong to be fast;" "They are not ready for me;" "I have to slow down in order to survive;" "People resent me for being fast. . .people get jealous that I have it easy," etc.

These people often grow up being impatient. They may have been ready to *go for it* and *get on with it*, but the delivery team wasn't. They may have been ready to talk sooner and walk sooner, but their family had the belief system that went by the book. This person may later attract a mate in a relationship who takes a long time and is slow because they have the thought "I have to wait for others."

In some families where there was a history of "quick births," the doctor may decide that the next birth must be "controlled." We have had clients who were *induced* for that reason; former babies in that family came "too fast" according to someone's standards.

These people feel "slowed down" inappropriately and unfairly. They were naturally quick already in the womb and then very shocked when they had to be stopped because former siblings were fast. They often end up with the thought: "People stop my power," or, if the obstetrician was male, they may have the thought specifically "Men stop my power." Therefore, in a relationship with a man, a woman with this mind-set may feel held back and controlled and weakened. Of course they attract a man like the obstetrician, who would try to control them by holding them back. We call this "Reverse Induction" cases since the motives for the induction are just opposite of most inductions.

If the baby is coming "too fast," and the doctor has not yet arrived, the nurses may try to hold the baby back by crossing the mother's legs. We are surprised as to how many cases like this we have seen in rebirthing. These people are often very angry and frustrated at being *held back*. In their lives they are often *blocked* and get *stuck*. They have to create some kind of *breakthrough*. In one case we knew, the person had to take up racing cars to prove that he could *keep going*. Another client we had needed to take up skin diving. Once she jumped, she had to keep going like the race car driver. She was trying to prove no one could stop her or hold her back.

In relationships, this person may attract a mate who will psychically hold her back. She thinks she needs this in order to survive; however she will resent it like crazy. People like this have a need to "break out" of their relationships. They may also suffer from claustrophobic feelings in life as a result of being stuck in the birth canal. "I'm stuck" is a common birth thought, which may create getting stuck in elevators, cars, or other small spaces. You could also feel smothered in a relationship, as well as trapped in general. You might feel "held back" in your career, not getting the promotions you desire. Or you could create a major business deal being "held up" at the last minute, leading to extreme frustration.

One graduate wrote to us,

Even though my birth was normal, I still felt very rushed. That is the way I am in life, running constantly, rushed and nervous. . . . My relationship is often a projection of my birth—I feel controlled, vulnerable, like I have no choices. I am rushed, out of control, and told what to do.

Another student reports,

I was born forty-five minutes after my mother got to the hospital. I am always quick and in a rush—everything has to be known as of yesterday. I create men leaving me and I know (naturally) it's because my dad left. Sometimes I feel closed in, trapped. . .mostly, I'm afraid to be vulnerable. My mother keeps me at a distance. . . .

One client remembers,

My mother was rushed into the delivery room ahead of other women in labor because she had fast labor. The birth itself was very quick and uncomplicated. Now I feel guilty about stepping on other people's toes or moving ahead of them; I feel resentful of women because my mother let me be taken away from her. I don't feel very nourished in my relationships because I was the only child in my family not breastfed; I feel competitive with other women for men's affection and attention—rivalry with my two sisters. I feel uncomfortable asking for attention. . .so I am careful to appear innocent of getting the attention I get. I am addicted to sensual and sexual pleasure because the passage through the birth canal was the most pleasurable part of my relationship with my mother and I miss her love.

One young lady recalls,

My birth was hurried. I was born in a taxi cab. I remember the coldness, the fear of death, the harsh words from the midwife to my mother. Now I am a terrible procrastinator, and my lateness is followed by intense guilt and despair. I have discipline, but no purpose; I'm tired a lot and sleep excessively, and I feel great sadness with lots of unreturned love. I'm forced to make last minute decisions. I'm really vulnerable and influenced by other people choosing for me. I'm self-centered. I hold back. Men desert me! I don't feel I can have a satisfying relationship. I want everything yesterday. I want it now. I don't feel worthy. I let it happen and have it done to me. I make last minute choices. . . . I must have direction in my life. I can't handle shouting. I'm courageous and accept openly. I want to accept the truth and run like hell!

Yet another student reports,

Because my birth was relatively quick and easy, I have found it easy to be successful quickly at new things which truly motivate me. I also felt that I had to subdue my self-expression even while in the birth canal so as not to "rock the boat" with the hospital staff. This tendency continues now. I was born at Doctor's Hospital across from the Mayor's mansion in a wealthy neighborhood, then lived for eight months one block from Carnegie Hall; so I've always been "at home" with public figures and artists.

One young man finds unusual events are easy:

I was born quickly, but my parents, nurses, and doctors panicked. I simply decided to do it now. As an adult, before something happens, I worry and think about everything that can possibly happen. When the event actually happens, I slip into it very naturally and do whatever needs to be done and usually have a very good time of it. After almost any unusual event I often say, "That was easy!"

Another graduate of the LRT writes,

I was wanted. I was born one and a half years after my sister. She had a long and difficult labor. I came very fast. My parents panicked and raced to the hospital. The doctor and nurses panicked, gave my mother a shot just as I was coming out. She passed out and I appeared. I thought she didn't care about me so I raised a fuss just to get her attention. Ever since then I have had the thought that I have to perform to get women's attention. But if I do, then I am creating a fake character and they will find out sooner or later and leave me because I lied.

* * *

One "held back" person reports,

My mother broke her foot just before I was born and was in a cast at my birth. I was named after my grandfather who had died. There were several false labors. Then I was held in; the nurses either held or tied my mother's legs together. Then I was pulled out; I almost died—I came out blue. I couldn't breathe well and was put in an incubator for three days. . . .

I have tremendous separation anxiety with people. I feel that I have to break through a wall of distance and can't. I have a strong fear of rejection and self-expression. . . . I think that my husband holds me back and since he was induced, I pull him along. My parents had financial problems at my birth, and I used to have financial worries. I still feel some scarcity and jealousy around love. I feel left out a lot. I don't think I deserve my husband's attention because I drain him emotionally and financially. I have a lot of fear around men. I think men like women who are helpless. I feel guilt and embarrassment in writing this. . ."

Another such case recalls,

I was held back for two hours so the doctor could sleep. Then they used forceps. I have created waiting for men all my life. I have deep anger at men. My parents wanted a boy. I was cold and scared and strangled when I was born and the doctor popped my back trying to get me to breathe and my spine has been slightly crooked all my life. I felt very out of control and didn't want to be here. I came very close to suicide a few years ago and sometimes I still don't want to be here. I did not feel safe in my body until I started rebirthing. Oh, yes, one of my nurses in the delivery room was wearing Jungle Gardenia perfume and I always have started to choke every time I smelled it all my life!

A rebirther remembers,

Normal birth? Nothing special except the obstetrician was late. My mother was told to close her legs; she can't be ready now! Inside I say, oh, that's how it works: people will tell me when I'm ready. I will wait. Wait, this is getting frightening! But there is somehow the thought that it is safer in here than it is out there. My mother was embarrassed to be pregnant. She thought she was ugly. To be seen is to be hurt, humiliated. I can't be seen. I won't come out. That is why I didn't want to come out of the womb. It isn't safe to be seen. As I come out, it becomes reality. The hurt. The humiliation. But the contradiction. I have to get out or die. What a choice, stay and die; leave and die. There must be a higher thought. To be born is to choose life. It is obvious. It is a fear of being hurt, of hurting another, guilt. Guilt demands punishment. Struggle. . .

One young lady writes,

My mom was separated. She had three boys already. My father's father drove her to the hospital, left her in an elevator and said, "Bye!" It was early morning. The MD was late. The nurses tried to hold my mom's legs together. Finally, the doctor arrived in suit and tie and I was born, quick and easy. My mom was glad I was a girl. . . .

I've always felt separate from people and worry that they'll leave if I get too close. I mistrust a lot and have a lot of helplessness. I feel like I can't let people know what's going on with me (like Mom being without a husband) for fear of judgment or humiliation. I did something wrong. I don't ask for help, like Mom; I have to do it alone, like Mom; I need to be strong, like Mom. Sometimes I feel like I relate wrong. I fear that my love will create separation. . .

A SUMMARY OF FAST BIRTHS:

(1) Most of the time they feel rushed and nervous, always running;
(2) they feel their mates rush them and they have no choice about it;
(3) they sometimes feel guilty about stepping on the toes of others;
(4) they often want everything in a hurry;
(5) often they have lots of energy—maybe even hyperactive;
(6) they mention they are occasionally good athletes;
(7) some of them mention they find it easy to succeed quickly;
(8) often they want and crave speed, and their mates cannot keep up;
(9) one said "unusual events are easy for me."

A SUMMARY OF HELD BACK BIRTHS:

(1) They often wait until things get frightening;
(2) they feel a need to break through a "wall of resistance" and cannot;
(3) they feel helpless;
(4) often their mate "holds them back" in relationships;
(5) they feel unsafe in their body;
(6) some complain of a "crooked spine;"
(7) some have the thought "I can't get what I want when I want it;"
(8) some have the thought "In order to prevent others from holding me back, I have to leave."

AFFIRMATIONS FOR FAST/HELD BACK BIRTHS

(1) *Time is on my side.*
(2) *I'm always at the right place at the right time successfully engaged in the right activity.*
(3) *My time is the right time.*
(4) *I'm always on time for myself.*
(5) *I forgive myself for thinking I had to satisfy other people's schedules to survive.*
(6) *It's safe to go fast.*
(7) *It's safe to take my time.*
(8) *The more I take my time, the more time I have to take.*
(9) *Slowly is holy!*
(10) *I no longer need to create obstacles to overcome.*
(11) *I no longer need to feel resistance in order to make it.*
(12) *People support me in choosing what I want when I want.*
(13) *All my arrivals and departures are easy and pleasurable.*
(14) *It's safe for me to go for it now!*
(15) *I forgive others when they are not ready for me.*
(16) *I am always ready for what comes next.*
(17) *It's safe to be ready.*

Chapter 12

PREMATURE/LATE

Are you an early riser? A late bloomer? An eager beaver? A procrastinator? Your entire relationship to time may be a function of the time of your birth. Are you a nocturnal person? An afternoon delight? It might be more than biorhythms. *The time of the day you were born might be the most traumatic part of every day for you.* If you were born in the morning, don't be surprised if early morning rush hours are particularly hard on your spirit.

If you were born significantly early or late, it may have contributed to a life-long pattern of being ahead of yourself or falling behind and having to catch up. Ideally, a baby is born in his or her own time, not to satisfy his parents' or doctor's schedule. The urgency adults bring to the birth process is largely a result of the urgency of their own births, an urgency best described by the phrase, "Let's hurry up and get it over with!" The unborn child can feel a victim of some unseen time-keeper even when he doesn't know the meaning of time.

We are neurotic about time from Day 1. Phrases like "time's running out," "a prisoner of time," "it's about time," indicate an essentially unhappy relationship with time. Often the feeling of "living on borrowed time" causes one's unconscious death urge to be activated from the first breath of life, contributing to making life feel like a race to the wire, even though that very wire is the terminal you least desire.

If a baby comes unusually early, why?

If there are unusual delays, why?

In many cases, we have rebirthed people who chose to be born early because: the mother was ill or frightened; there was a previous miscarriage, abortion, or still-born; he felt unwanted; he was just very eager to get on with his life. Of course, most of these reasons can apply to late births too.

An important affirmation is, "I am always in the right place at the right time, successfully engaged in the right activity."

Another is, "My time is the right time!" And, "Time is on my side!"

In relationships, a child born premature can either always be rushing his partner, thereby acting out his own birth (while playing the obstetrician for his partner); or he might be preoccupied with taking his time to compensate for the lack of time he had in the womb. You can be an eager beaver if you were born with enthusiasm, ahead of your time, as it were, and have trouble communicating to us more normal, slow folk; you might live life in the fast lane because for you it seems like the only way to go. On the other hand, if a child came early to protect his mother and/or avoid anticipated mishaps, he could be extremely cautious in relationships, his mind very quick but his body slow to react.

If you were put in an incubator, you would tend to have double separation trauma. You came out of the womb only to be put in another artificial womb—it may seem hopeless for you ever to connect with other human beings. You may have more difficulty than most people in letting go, completing old relationships, feeling touched or seen. You might wear thick glasses or simply feel like your being is surrounded by walls of glass.

We once had a client born over a month late. In fact, his mother told him he took eleven months. Of course, she wasn't a mathematician, but he got the notion that he was very late. This is a man with big ideas, always one step ahead of his competitors, who lives his life as though he's making up for lost time. At the same time, since the reason he was late was because his body was big, and he didn't want to hurt his mother, he is very loving and protective by nature, sometimes causing him to suppress his aliveness to support those he loves.

We know many such cases, where adults are stuck in the future because their relationship with time is confused from birth.

Late babies, or extremely long labors, can produce relationships that feel very stuck, delayed, held back. We know a woman whose mother was in labor with her for two days. She is constantly late for appointments, especially with loved ones. Professionally, she switched careers in mid-life and was a late-bloomer.

Some babies delayed coming out because their parents wanted a child of the opposite sex. They wanted to postpone the inevitable disappointment, which can lead to stalling tactics later in life.

When you master time, you learn that you are the only one you are ever late for. You were never intended to live your life according to someone else's schedule. Your life works best when you follow your own intuitive rhythm, choosing where to be and when, depending on where your heart takes you. Moreover, your rhythm doesn't hurt anyone else; in fact, it is in harmony with all of life itself.

Can you imagine the Mississippi River trying to flow at a speed that would please the Gulf of Mexico? The ole Miss just does her own thing, and you never hear the Gulf complain.

Mastering your relationship with time is mastering life itself—getting off the birth/death cycle, flowing in the immortal continuum of ever-present now-ness.

* * *

PREMATURE & "INCUBATOR"

In the case of a premature birth, we would try to find out in the rebirthing why this person came out of the womb early. There is usually some specific reason that he or she did not naturally stay in for the full time. Perhaps the mother was sick. . .often the "vibes" inside the mother were not good, and the person actually felt unsafe staying inside. Usually the delivery team and family were worried about the baby's survival. These babies often develop thoughts like "I am weak," "I am too small," "I am frail," and/or "I can't make it."

The incubator period produces a considerable amount of trauma. For one thing, consider the baby's feeding issues: Since the baby had to be fed intravenously, this is a problem with such small veins. Therefore, the needles are usually placed in the scalp and feet. In order to keep from having the needles come out, the baby usually is *tied down*. When you imagine the newborn being tied down inside of a box, you can see why this baby usually ends up with a thought "I'm *helpless*" or "I can't help it." This may become a life-long pattern.

Often these people grow up with a "wall" of some kind around them, which they think they need in order to survive. Tiny babies often are overweight adults and vice versa. Since being overweight was a problem at birth, they overcompensate.

This "wall," then, can take the form of being overweight which is used for protection; or this wall can also be a "psychic wall" difficult for others to penetrate. Very often a premature has the thought: "*Look, but don't touch,*" so they unconsciously keep people away, especially affection-wise and sexually.

Once we had a client that kept having the following dream: She would see hands coming through clouds. These hands would be coming at her. She worked out a lot of her incubator trauma in these dreams. (In nursing school, the way we bathed premies was to put on gloves, put a bowl of warm water in the incubator, and put the baby in the little bowl. It was astonishing just how these tiny beings could fit in a small bowl!)

Usually a premature-incubator person has to be rebirthed double. They not only have to be rebirthed out of the womb; but also rebirthed out of the incubator.

There is a tendency to set up a relationship as the incubator. The relationship then becomes a life-death type of situation to which the person clings desperately in an "unhealthy" way, even though they may think their health depends on it. If you encourage them to free themselves from it, it may appear to them you are nearly killing them.

Sometimes prematures are physically unhealthy. They may even look as though they are not fully born. By changing the thoughts, "I am weak and helpless," they can make a lot of progress healthwise. We usually acknowledge them for having such a strong life urge that they could survive incredible odds. Although their life urge was weak and created them barely making it, on the other hand we try to emphasize that part of their life urge that did pull them through, and we reinforce that. Another thing that really helps is encouraging them to go for spiritual nourishment. Body work is also very important.

These people must be encouraged to see that they can be independent and survive. The trouble is that they tend to attract people to be in relationships with that need someone dependent on them (which reinforces incubator neurosis). Becoming very aware of these patterns is the first step, and consciously working on them in the rebirthing process has produced remarkable results.

Sometimes it is very easy to get drawn into the fear of hurting this kind of person and unconsciously reinforcing their "frailness" by being overprotective. In some cases, a healing may come when they are actually made to *move* physically, that is, from their house (the incubator) to another house, another job, or even another town.

A now happily married (and currently pregnant) client reports:

I was premature—born at six and a half months. I was put in an incubator for seven weeks—my parents visited me every day and were 'willing' me to live. My father was particularly afraid and sad that I might not make it. When they brought me home, they kept me in a separate room with a lot more windows and wore surgical masks to visit me. The obstetrician was frightened—I was so small—and rushed me to the nurse to go to the nursery. My mother was thirty-six and my father forty-two and my sister (by my mother's first marriage) was sixteen. I felt like I had to make it on my own.

The way my birth affects my relationships is that I seem to get only so close and then create a glass wall. I never seem totally bonded with a man. I want to get married but create men who don't want to, or that I don't think are good enough. I have been very independent and want to prove that I can do it myself financially. I love having lots of people around and being the focus of attention, yet feel embarrassed when it happens. I seem to frighten lots of men like I did my father and my obstetrician. We end up in a look-don't-touch relationship.

A former client, now a happily married staff member, reports:

I was two weeks premature and only weighed two pounds, four ounces. My parents separated when I was in the womb. I was plunged in cold water to get me breathing. For two to three days I was in an iron lung, then in an incubator.

The way my birth has affected my relationship is I've always felt more comfortable alone. I like people, but feel like I'm imposing or not wanted. I tend to rush into relationships then wonder why I'm there. I feel comfortable and close to women, but don't understand intimacy or bonding with men. I tend to keep myself aloof and separate a lot, invisibility equals safety. I get "plugged-in" when I feel I'm not getting what I want, so I don't ask—do it myself. I try very hard to please in overcompensation for feeling like an imposition. It's difficult for me to surrender totally, especially in sex: I fear men will hurt me when I'm vulnerable, or be insensitive. I hate being cold, feel unloved, uncared for, manipulated. Life is unfair and disappointing, depressing and sad.

Another client reports,

I was two months premature and spent three months in an incubator.

The ways my birth affects my relationship are: I'm not touched enough. I feel a lot of anger in relationships. I want love but don't know how to receive it. I'm very independent, I love being in love. I want to be touched and held but I didn't know how to accept it before rebirthing. Now I know how to accept. I used to carry my incubator around with me for forty years. I am now shedding it.

One "war baby" writes:

I was born during the Japanese occupation of Manila, 6-16-42. I was manually induced, premature—dry. My parents called me their "blackout" baby. I was the fourth of eight children, the only one born abroad, in a Red Cross camp schoolhouse.

My birth affects my relationships in that I am afraid of relationships—afraid they will hurt; I am too immature for relationships; I will lose myself; I will die; I don't like men; I think I should please men. Sometimes I overcompensate by feeling superior and acting that out. I don't want to see myself. I would have to be there; I would have to live if I wanted relationships.

A friend tells us:

I was premature, it was a dry birth. I was put in an incubator, separated from my mother; I almost died from dehydration. I was delivered not by the regular doctor but a friend of the family (a doctor) who happened to be there.

The way my birth affects my relationships is that I feel I have to be separate to survive—"incubator trauma." Being separated from my mother caused such profound sadness and pain that I said I would never ever again risk that withdrawal of love. I would never suffer abandonment again. Indeed, I would be able to do it myself, independently: I would "go it alone." In terms of bonding with people, I have many close, tender, affectionate friends, and yet the intimacy and surrender of a loving sexual relationship frightens me.

Being premature, often I feel excited and empowered to move or make a decision, and then afterwards, to be overwhelmed with the thoughts of:
> *I can't make it,*
> *I'm not ready,*
> *I goofed.*

A former member of our staff writes:

I was an incubator baby—separated from my family for two to three weeks. I was never touched by my mother until I went home (two to three weeks later). I was premature by at least two months, not planned. Obviously the timing of my birth a surprise—no indication I would be premature until it happened. Born at 3:15 AM very small—three and a half pounds—and that created urgency and intensity in birth and concern over life/death.

The way my birth affects my relationships is that they always seem to be intense and at times, particularly in male relationships, I feel a sense of urgency over where the relationship is headed—almost as if having to reach some kind of completion as soon as it's begun. I very much feel I have to wait for men to be ready to love me and I have to stay separate from them when intense, loving feelings, especially mine, come up in the relationship. I notice that the time I always think is appropriate is somewhere between two and three weeks; then I can be with them again. Anytime sooner feels like the relationship will die (and I've also created this). I generally create relationships with people who are not demonstrative about loving feelings—they don't touch or hug, and my husband did not find it easy to touch/hug. I always judge myself for going too fast in relationships; it seems I know too soon about the relationship I want—who and when. I like to be around people who stay up late—not just a little late like midnight or 1 AM, but more like 2 or 3 AM.

Another client, who just made it, shares:

My birth was premature and dry. I was not breastfed and became dehydrated (I almost died). I was lightly drugged and put in an incubator.

My thought is that I cannot be intimate with the ones I love; therefore, I never have sex with my friends. I find that the most exciting sexual moments are shared more with strangers or acquaintances. When the situation evolves from sexual to intimate, I panic, I flee, and then make them wrong. I also have the thought that the ones I love either can't or don't nourish me, as I was never breastfed. It affects my working life drastically in that I work with people I love, the pay is meager, and if I want to be paid well, I have to do a job I dislike or that it is unfulfilling.

I also drink a lot with my closest friends. Alcohol (particularly white wine) and marijuana seem to be intimately woven into our social interactions. I know that the hospital staff administered a drug to my mother at my birth.

I also have the thought that women abandon me and do not nourish me. But then I have a matching one that says "Men hurt me." This is a no-win situation. This is why I have a commitment to breathing this out of my body and subconscious mind.

Performing for love or performing for attention is another characteristic of being in an incubator. Mowing the lawn perfectly, being a "puffect little boy." I got good grades and was paid for it.

Another graduate of the Loving Relationships Training writes,

I was a Preemie; there was a sense of great urgency in the delivery room. "I'm

OK," I thought, but I couldn't communicate it. I was forceably breathed by machine, and in the incubator for two weeks; my father was not present; I was raised by a single parent.

The way birth affected my relationships was that I felt a sense of anxiety and tension early in my relationships, with men especially. I had a very difficult time in asking for what I needed and resented it when I didn't get it. I felt that men were not there for me, were not to be trusted and would leave me. It was difficult to bond with men or women, and I had a strong need to do things myself. It felt very comfortable to be alone, although if alone when I don't want to be, I experienced a lot of sadness and anger.

I give deep thanks for healing of these negative thoughts and patterns through rebirthing and the Loving Relationships Training.

The following is a report from a long-suffering woman,

It was a long labor—I was induced because the contractions weren't strong enough. After induction there were several very strong contractions and then nothing for two hours. Then I was born. Mom was anesthetized: forceps were used to pull me out. I was a low birth weight so I was put in an incubator for two days. Mother breastfed me, so I did come out of the incubator for that.

The way my birth affects my relationships are—Long labor seems to affect my relationships whenever I am trying to solve an issue. I want to talk long about the problem, I seem to drag out the conversations. Induced relates to my husband and others always telling me to hurry up, that I'm too late and not ready on time. Incubator feeling of not being able to be heard, so in relationships I'm not understood. I have to keep repeating myself. I say something and it is almost like I never said it. My mom got tired during labor, and they used a drug to induce the labor. It feels like the ways I recreate this in relationships is needing help or need to think of clever ways not to have the relationship get stuck. My mom was anesthetized, and my partner tends to be anesthetized during our relationship. Since I felt I hurt my mom, I have guilt and try to protect my mate, not being myself, so as not to hurt him.

A student of ours writes,

I was born in a hospital, at night—my mother was in fear and feeling alone, out of control; I was three weeks late. There was a pre-war baby who died in utero before me, probably was a boy. They said I was wanted. I was a post-war baby.

I am usually late to whatever I am going to. Keep people waiting. Have a great fear of keeping people waiting. It is very difficult for me to get somewhere on time and not feel pressured, uncomfortable, and "on the spot."

I have a tremendous resistance to being close to my mother. Lot of hatred for her. Lot of "leave me alone"—"go away!" "Please leave my life permanently." In other relationships, I always want to leave, not be touched, be by myself. Don't like sleeping in the same bed with my husband. Love sleeping alone—feel alone at night. I don't trust it when people tell me they love me. My mother told me she loved me, that is why she was doing all the unconscious things she did. I don't feel supported in my close relationships. I hate hospitals. I constantly feel out of control and in fear in most relationships. I didn't want to become a mother and went through tremendous resistance to pregnancy, conception, labor, and motherhood.

One graduate of the LRT writes,

I was twenty days late. They thought I was twins, then I was to be breech. At the last minute I turned. Mother had a hard birth. She said she took ex-lax and I was almost born in a "slop jar" but she still had a long labor—twenty-four hours.

The way my birth affects my relationships are: I was covered with "poop"— I'm a piece of shit! My father was out drinking and was drunk when I was born. My mother wouldn't let him see me. I was born the day before his birthday— didn't wait long enough. I was a "duty" child. My sisters didn't want another baby—I was number four. The main ways my birth affects my relationships are: I'm not worthy; I'm not wanted; I'm not loved; men are never there when I need them.

Another graduate reports,

The only thing that I know about my birth is that my mother said that I was like a monster, crying and not smiling and being nice as babies should. I feel I had a great struggle being born although I was a normal birth.

I came two weeks late. My mother was very young and not ready to care for a baby. I believe that she was repelled by breast feeding and her milk soon dried up. I know she did not want to hold me because I always feel that people don't want to touch me, that there is something wrong with me. I know that all my life I have been looking for the bonding that I never had so I expect too much from relationships. Without that bonding I have felt awkward and separate and alone in this life.

I feel that there is something wrong with me and if someone tries to love me they will find that out. I have always been afraid to commit myself to a relationship. I want too much and always bring about struggle and rejection (either by me or my partner). I feel inadequate as a woman, because my mother was not able to give me warmth and nourishment, so I feel I cannot give that to men. I feel very jealous of other women because I feel they can give something that I can't. So I can never rest and feel comfortable and secure in relationships.

A SUMMARY OF PREMATURE/LATE:

(1) They feel like intrusions;
(2) they feel ahead of everyone else;
(3) they feel immature in relationships;
(4) they are extremely vulnerable;
(5) often they are small and feel insignificant.

Incubator births can feel:
(1) Separate and alone;
(2) afraid of touch;
(3) observed and judged.

Long labors can feel:
(1) Slow, frustrated, in pain;
(2) they are disappointments;
(3) they keep everyone waiting;
(4) they hurt people;
(5) life is tough and a struggle;
(6) they are late bloomers.

AFFIRMATIONS FOR PREMATURE/LATE:

(See all affirmations for fast/held-back as well.)
      (1) I have everything I need to get everything I want.
      (2) I am just the right size.
      (3) I am enough, I have enough, I do enough.
      (4) I'm safe at any speed.
      (5) I'm safe at any time.
      (6) It's safe to be early.
      (7) It's safe to be late.
      (8) I no longer have to rush to make it.
      (9) I no longer have to go slow to make it.
      (10) I forgive my delivery team for rushing me.
      (11) The divine plan of my life unfolds on schedule!

Chapter 13

CESARIAN

In a sense, "cesarians" have it easier. They don't have to plow through the birth canal to make it; nor do they have to be as guilty about causing their mothers pain. A simple incision does the trick. And nowadays, a c-section is a minor surgical procedure which makes birth quicker and easier for mother, doctor, and child.

In a sense!

The cesarian child, however, often suffers from interruption syndrome since his original direction in life was rudely interrupted by the obstetrician. (Nowadays, there is a proliferation of cesarians, often simply to please the doctor, fit his schedule, his golf game, whatever.)

He will often grow into a headstrong adult who insists on doing things his own way, often at his own expense. At the same time, the more he insists on going his own way in life, the more likely he is to attract unforseen interruptions blocking his path. He seems to want to make the journey through the birth canal he never made in the first place. He knows he knows how to do it, if only everyone else would leave him alone!

But they never do. People get in the way. Often, when cesarians are being rebirthed, they will create constant interruptions to upset themselves, evoking the confusion they experienced when coming out. A cesarian's relationships tend to be characterized by conflicts of will, changes of heart and mind, and constant disruptions. We've known several cesarian couples, and usually they are looking for someone outside the relationship to tell them which way to go in life, then resenting it and doing the opposite. If one partner is cesarian and the other is not, the latter can be set up to be the obstetrician—which happens in many relationships.

Support can be a major issue for cesarians. On the one hand, they want it desperately; on the other hand, they mistrust it and see all support as manipulation, interference, and opposition.

"I want to do it my way!" is the cry of the cesarian, at the same time thinking, "I better get some help or I'll never get out of this." The cesarian's double bind produces confusion at every crossroad of life. Let him drive a car, give him clear directions, and the journey will become a major obstacle course. You say "Turn left," and he'll turn right. You can bet on it. You say "North," and he'll go south.

Cesarians crave physical affection. Because they never received the initial massage the walls of the birth canal provide, they need a lot of extra hugging, holding, and cuddling as children. If they don't get it as children, they may still need what seems like an excess of caressing as adults.

Cesarians do have the potential for seeing the easy way out. When they relax into this knowledge, they are a vast storehouse for shortcuts in life. Once they get over their guilt for not doing it the hard way in the first place, they can enjoy the innocence of their own intuitive know-how. They can save us all a lot of time and energy.

Every birth contains an unknown gift!

One of our students reports,

At my birth the doctors came into the womb with a knife to get me out. I felt like my space was invaded without my permission. Today I feel that sometimes people come up and want to get inside my space, and I don't want them there. I feel the same inability to effectively communicate to them to leave me alone. Since I was removed from my mother without her touching me, I felt very rejected. Most of my life I was afraid that if I really wanted to be with someone, they would send me away, so I was always afraid of being rejected.

I felt very angry and humiliated at my birth and that the doctors and nurses didn't receive my communication. My primary relationship today has difficulty hearing and is always asking me to repeat myself. I get angry when I have to repeat what I said.

Since I didn't get out of the womb by myself, I get afraid that emergencies are going to happen, and I need to be surrounded by people capable of saving me.

I thought I hurt my mother at birth, and I am always thinking people are accusing me of causing them pain.

One graduate writes of her cesarian birth,

The circumstances of my parents' relationship at conception and birth definitely have affected my relationships. Following my brother's vaginal stillbirth, my parents separated. They came together again to have a baby (me) to heal their relationship. Inside the womb I felt anxious and afraid like I had to get out or die like my brother. I kicked my foot and broke the water five weeks early. I was born via c-section, and my mother's first words after my birth to the obstetrician were, "I consider you next to God." And then I was taken away from her for twenty-four hours. I screamed in the nursery all the time, and when brought to my mother to nurse, I'd fall asleep.

Those first decisions have affected the relationships I have with people in my life. I feel I hurt people because people have to die so I can live (my brother), and my mother was hurt at my birth. I feel guilty because I caused the separation from my mother (and God), and because my birth was so easy for me.

I also create struggle with people because I struggled with the obstetrician and the nurses at my birth. I consciously became a nurse to help people because my mother was hurt by insensitive nurses. My unconscious reason was because I was afraid I had hurt people. I also married a doctor (who I struggle with—doctors are next to God) and am presently a birth assistant. In my relationship with myself, I frequently feel isolated, depressed, and unloved. When I ask for help, it's usually by screaming helplessly, and when not responded to, I cry myself to sleep.

A staff member recalls,

I was transverse lay, cesarian, anesthesia, brief time in incubator, and asleep first three days after birth from anesthesia.

I have great difficulty going directly towards people/careers that I really want. Even very big decisions are made very quickly—cesarian style. Once I arrive in a relationship, city, or career, it is often not clear how I got there, and I spend some time in the early stages of relationship somewhat unconscious. I do feel that there is sometimes a bit of a wall (incubator) between myself and others.

One client reports,

I was cesarian, born with rickets. Anesthesia was used and there was subsequent maternal damage and hysterectomy. Having convinced myself that I hurt people and they probably wouldn't like me anyway, it's been my policy to stay away, to create emotional distance and let passion and sensation take the place of loving trust.

As a person who has been yanked out, untimely ripped, I have a feeling that I yank myself out of relationships, and I've walked out of a couple of truly fine ones and dozens of ones of lesser magnitude. I feel unlovable and selfconscious that there's something wrong with me, perhaps because I was born with rickets and must have been something of a disappointment to a family that prefers perfection.

The presence of anesthesia during the cesarian section probably has a lot to do with the fact that I stayed high on pot for fifteen years and drank daily for most of that time. Maybe the lesson was that consciousness is painful.

A cesarian graduate of the LRT writes,

During any relationship that I have, I immediately feel as if I am at the effect of the other person. I create men to be my obstetrician. Being smothered is a feeling I usually get when there is love present, so I feel the need to leave my body. I got a lot of anesthesia during my birth, so when I am touched, my body feels numb with anesthesia. I never feel as if I can do anything myself, and when I do, my body goes numb, and it's as if I never accomplished anything. During my birth, I felt a knife come to my back, but not touch me, so often I feel that support will kill me, and I am suspicious of love from other people. . .even myself, sometimes.

During my birth, I believed I was going to decide to be born when I wanted to, but the doctor decided instead, so during sex when I feel I am about to climax, I feel that it will be taken away.from me, so instead of being disappointed by my mate, I cut off myself first by going unconscious.

A former client writes,

My birth script was cesarian delivery because of the cord being wrapped around my neck and not being able to come down the birth canal. My mother was anesthetized, and I was separated because of an infection.

The way that my birth has affected my relationships is that I have often felt strangled and overpowered by women, yet wanted to be rescued, or "pulled out." Also, my relationships have been mostly struggle and pain. I have often felt like I couldn't do it right, or my way wasn't right. I also have an obsession with vaginas. I buy lots of magazines with pictures of vaginas. Lately, I have thought that I wasn't good enough to have it easy at birth, or to have an easy, lasting relationship, because I thought that eventually I would be separated from the ones that I love.

Another staff member recalls,

I was stuck near Mom's pelvic bone. I was cesarian; turmoil, confusion, and anxiety surrounding my birth. I was unplanned; my birth was difficult, painful, *and rushed. Mom was weak and undernourished, heavily anesthetized, and not really there. I was not breastfed for long—separation not only at birth, but both parents worked a lot and weren't home when I was an infant. Mom and Dad had an arranged marriage, and there was a lot of uncertainty in their relationship and arguments—guilt in hurting Mom at birth.*

The main way my birth affects my relationships is that I find it more difficult to breathe in a relationship or when I'm with people than when I'm alone. There is a problem with not enough space, time, and air to breathe. Sometimes I just want to get out of there. The turmoil, confusion, and anxiety that existed not only about my birth, but also in regard to my newly married parents, keep manifesting in my own relationships. Most of my loving relationships happen by surprise and when I'm not expecting to become involved. I usually manifest women with small breasts, and to this degree, I feel undernourished. Also, my loved ones seem to be anesthetized (at times) when I want to make love or play.

I always seem to have to wait for things to happen, and then I usually feel rushed by my partner. I also feel lots of struggle and arguments in some of my relationships. I have lots of fear in saying no, especially to women. Because Mom and Dad were always working, they had very little time to nourish me, and so this also happens in my relationships where my partner is too busy working or is too tired to play.

In conclusion, my claustrophobia keeps me separate to a degree, and, in addition, I need support and assistance from friends in my relationships—to be hauled out of problems and turmoils when I feel stuck.

Another graduate reports,

Eight babies were being born at the same time I was, so I'm always concerned with others' births—I want them to get born with me.

For three days, I was asleep, and I astrally traveled around the hospital seeing how things could be better, so I always want to heal systems, like educational systems, etc.

Being cesarian, it always feels like I'm moving slowly, and then all of a sudden, it's done and everything is finished.

Being asleep the first three days, I never know how anything gets done. Things just seem to get done psychically.

I rarely go straight for what I want, so I go sideways, and then it just happens.

SUMMARY OF CESARIAN BIRTHS:

(1) They suffer from "interruption syndrome;"
(2) often, they have a fear of knives and sharp instruments;
(3) they can't do it by themselves;

(4) they resent others manipulating them;

(5) they often crave touching;

(6) often they are indirect in their communications;

(7) they tend to think they do it wrong;

(8) they are easily confused;

(9) they find it difficult to make decisions;

(10) they're kind of "damned if they do, damned if they don't;"

(11) they have a hard time completing things.

AFFIRMATIONS FOR CESARIAN BIRTHS:

(1) *I am innocent.*

(2) *My way is the right way.*

(3) *I can always find the easy way.*

(4) *I'm right in the first place.*

(5) *All my interruptions are for my highest good.*

(6) *I forgive my mother completely.*

(7) *It's safe to do things differently.*

(8) *I forgive myself for doing things differently.*

(9) *I deserve all the touching and holding I desire.*

(10) *I'm always in the right place at the right time.*

(11) *It's safe to be in my body.*

(12) *I can trust my intuition.*

(13) *It's safe for me to complete things.*

Chapter 14

TRANSVERSE LIE

This means the baby is lying sideways, the head facing left or right, the feet the opposite. The baby is not facing the birth canal. This is an extreme medical emergency, usually requiring cesarian delivery. Sometimes the doctor will try to turn the baby manually from the outside. This is extremely painful to the mother and baby and often not successful.

As rebirthers, we would again try to find out why this person was going in the *wrong direction*. Usually the person definitely did not want to come out and/or got confused and "lost" in trying to find the way out. These people often have the thought "I need to go in the wrong direction in order to survive." They consequently are in the "wrong" careers. . .and "wrong" relationships. They stay too long in situations they should have gotten out of. They keep people waiting. They are either "stuck" where they are or are moving and moving and moving. . .trying to get out but not really getting anywhere, depending on which phase of the birth they are currently acting out.

The truth is, we have had only a few of these kinds of people in our practice, since it is such a rare condition. However, the process of working with them was quite dramatic and complicated. Often, these people come here with very important missions, which, at birth, they may not be ready to face, and they avoid this kind of power by turning. In one case, we were able to get the person "turned" and going in the right direction towards the career she came to do. . .but for quite some time afterwards, whenever we were with her, we moved and moved and moved. One time, over a two-week period, we had to move hotel rooms six different times! Every time we rode in a car with her, we would miss turns, get lost, and go around and around. We learned that in the delivery room, the doctor would come and try to turn her, then he would deliver another of the eight babies he had to deliver. Then he would return and try to turn her another notch. Being with her was like that. Since we were rebirthers (we were training her), we were very conscious of all this, able to talk about it, and she allowed us to rebirth her frequently through it. Tremendous progress was made once she made the initial turn.

Another case has been more difficult, and is still in process, because we have not been in the city where that client lives. We remember during one wet rebirth with him, he began spinning around almost violently in panic in the tub. It was so dramatic that we were able to experience what it was like to be his mother during these moments of delivery. Drugs seemed like the only hope of relieving the pain. The whole thing was like a *battle* between the mother and baby.

A transverse lie is not used to alignment. In a relationship, these people may form the habit of going in the opposite direction of their mate. This could include physically having to leave town if the relationship gets too close. If they cannot leave town, then they may have to oppose the other, since alignment is not something they can compute. Being out of alignment with the other feels "safer" and more familiar. This can be absolute "hell" on a relationship, unless both parties are very enlightened and understand what is going on in relation to their birth trauma.

Although the person desperately wants to be turned in the right direction and desperately wants to be aligned with another, this is at the same time terrifying, because of the pain and unfamiliarity. Although this all may be suppressed at the beginning of a relationship (therefore allowing some alignment and mutual direction in the beginning), then the love deepens and the birth trauma gets "activated." This is because love eventually brings up anything unlike itself; one partner may be suddenly shocked to see the other going in an opposite direction or actually leaving town for no apparent reason.

A transverse lie may have had so much pain around the attempted turns and related drugs that they sometimes "split off" from the body. In the cases we have worked with, being out of the body was more comfortable, safe, and pleasurable for them than being in the body.

It is almost as if these people have the thought "I can't be in the body and be safe." One had the thought "I can't love in the body." This was because he could not *feel* in his body due to the heavy drugs that had anesthetized him and because leaving the body was the escape mechanism used.

These people have formed such unusual thoughts that they are a mystery, and people are often lost as to how to relate to them.

In two particular cases we were very involved, trying desperately to figure out how to rebirth these people, how to help them, how to understand them. This is surely how the obstetrician must have felt. *"What do I do* to get this person out?" During one dry rebirth on a transverse lie, we had her align herself in a *very straight* line while we pulled on her feet trying to make her "straight." We kept saying loudly *STRAIGHT STRAIGHT STRAIGHT.* This produced a dramatic effect, and she said her energy felt aligned for the first time in her life after that.

One student recollects,

I was a transverse lie birth. All my relationships seem to be characterized by what I'd call a sense of misdirection. They seem to take me out of my way. I get stuck in them a lot, I struggle a lot, and I hate to be controlled or manipulated. Often it feels like my partner is trying to turn me or twist me in the opposite direction. I think I get lost in the middle a lot. Also, I just don't know how to leave a bad relationship.

Another client writes,

My birth was transverse lie and terribly painful for my mother. I think, as a result, I tend to be frozen in my relationships. I'm afraid that if I make any move at all, it will hurt my partner. Also, when I'm out driving with my partner, we get into terrible fights over what direction to take. We could kill each other over north and south, east and west. I hate back seat drivers.

Still another graduate reports,

I was all twisted up and didn't know which way to go. It was a transverse lie. When I came out, it was backwards. I can't do anything right. I'm always all caught up in the middle. I do things ass-backwards; I tend to try to squirm my way out of relationships. Women think I'm slippery, but I'm just trying to avoid friction. I hate confrontation. Often, it seems to me that everyone else is all twisted up and I'm the only one who's got things straight.

A SUMMARY OF TRANSVERSE LIE:

(1) They often complained of "going in the wrong direction" in regards to marriage and career;
(2) complained of confusion;
(3) complained of body pain;
(4) moving a lot;
(5) they avoid "tight squeezes;"
(6) they don't like to be controlled or manipulated;
(7) fear "alignment" in general.

AFFIRMATIONS FOR TRANSVERSE LIE BIRTHS:

(1) My body is a safe and pleasurable place to be.
(2) It's safe to move around.
(3) I can straighten myself out.
(4) I forgive people for trying to straighten me out.
(5) My way is the right way.
(6) I know where I'm going.
(7) It's safe for me to leave.
(8) It's safe for me to stay.
(9) I'm safe any which way I turn.
(10) I have a great sense of direction.
(11) I know where I'm going.
(12) It's a pleasure to move forward.
(13) I'm always free.
(14) The more I relax, the more space I create.

Chapter 15

DRUGS

When a mother is drugged at birth, the drugs cross the placenta (which acts more like a sieve than like a barrier), and the baby is "drugged" right at birth (and then we wonder why we have a drug problem in the world!). People who were drugged at birth are often born lifeless, and they spend their whole life in a "fog."

We were absolutely amazed to find that during the rebirth session, we could actually *"smell"* the drugs as they were breathed out. In one extreme case, Leonard Orr, founder of rebirthing, was rebirthing a psychiatrist in Paris with us. During the second half-hour of his breathing, not only could we smell the drugs, we were very dizzy and nearly passed out. We all spontaneously ran to the window and stuck our heads out for air! This man, by the way, had never had surgery or anesthesia after birth (it was therefore clearly drugs from birth). He said that after the rebirth, he felt alive for the first time in his life!

Clients who had a lot of anesthesia at birth often have the problem of "going unconscious" during rebirthing. A well-trained rebirther knows a lot of ways to get them through this, although it may take a while. People who were heavily anesthetized at birth generally take longer in the rebirthing process.

These people may also "go unconscious" in their relationships and at work. They often have trouble getting up in the morning. Their medicine cabinet may be full of drugs, or they may be "stoned" a lot on marijuana or even be drug addicts.

They may even recreate the need for surgery in their lives so that they can relive the "anesthesia" experience, subconsciously thinking they need it and can resolve it by "working it out" in reliving it.

On one occasion, we were rebirthing an experienced rebirther. Since he was a rebirther himself, he had the stamina and awareness we needed to study his "anesthesia-case." We were able to get him down to the exact thoughts he had had as the anesthesia took over his body. One minute he felt totally alive, ready to live fully and be born. The next minute, when the anesthesia crossed the placenta, he said, "I am turning to stone. My mother feels dead, too. . .have I killed her? . . .I cannot move. I am completely helpless. . . ." In his life, he had had a problem with helplessness. He was very brilliant but would periodically get very helpless. We were able to make a lot of progress with that problem in this particular rebirthing. We felt very sad during the rebirthing and cried when he recalled the experience of the anesthesia taking over his body. It seemed like he went from being totally alive to being *dead* right before our eyes. In our relationship with him, we would often see him "haze over" and go into something like "corpse consciousness." Fortunately, cold water rebirthing (which is *advanced* and should never be tried alone) helped him a great deal, and he became a very compassionate rebirther.

In rebirthing, we have had good results with people healing their drug addictions as it is often related to anesthesia. Unfortunately, we did not keep accurate records at the beginning of rebirthing and do not have statistical data. Rebirthers consider themselves to be spiritual guides, not scientists. Professional research, however, should and could be done in all areas of rebirthing, and one of the reasons we wrote this book was in the hopes of inspiring those interested in doing this research to come and join us.

Sometimes people who had anesthesia have thoughts like these: "I can't get what I want;" "I can't make it;" "I am helpless;" "I need to be drugged in order to survive;" "I am immobile;" "Aliveness is terrifying;" "I have to deaden things. . .tone things down;" or, "I can't be in control of my own body."

A typical "Anesthesia" type recollects,

The significant things about my birth were that my dad was out of town, my mother was very angry at me at the point when she decided to take general anesthesia and I decided I wanted out quick. It was my uncle's birthday which was an inconvenience to my family. And I felt hurt by my obstetrician.

This has caused me to project that all women want to suppress me (anesthesia), and that I cannot get what I want unless I am away from them. At the same time, I feel disapproval of my presence which has kept me from being a part of groups—fraternities, buddies, etc. And when I am a part—projecting disapproval onto it. I also concluded that my mother's anger was my fault, and she was a victim of men. Therefore, I feel guilty in the presence of women and attract "victim types" to hurt. I hated my mom for being mad at me, and I am constantly quick to get out of relationships and get on my own. Yet on my own and alone, I get hurt.

A young man thinks women are happier without him.

My mother was happy to be totally anesthetized and feel no pain. She wasn't there for me, and the doctor may have used forceps as a result. As a result of this, I don't count on anyone or expect that anyone will give me anything. My main social defense mechanism is withdrawal. I'll put up with things if I can just leave in protest, but if I'm told I can't withdraw, I get really violently angry. My whole social credo is that if people can't do anything good for each other, they can at least leave each other alone.

When I was born, I was very long, and my aunt, a nurse, who was present, made sarcastic remarks. I have always been afraid of being made fun of, unwilling to do things I'm afraid people will think are foolish, and I act aloof when I'm really scared inside.

I was taken away to the nursery and never bonded with my mother. I've been very emotionally cold and distant and never, until just recently, have known what it was like to love another person. My birth was painful and I'm pissed off and hostile a lot.

An LRT graduate writes,

My birth was easy; a typical hospital delivery. My mother was drugged with Twilight Sleep; she could see but not touch.

A way my birth affects my relationship is that I've tried to be invisible to cover the hurt I felt about not being able to connect with my mother. My mother had the thought "I'm not here." I've also felt disconnected and out of touch in many of my relationships. I tend to feel that I can't be with the people I love the most, since at my birth I had to be around hospital personnel instead of my mom. And last, but not least, unconsciousness and spaciness which seem to be coming up strongly while I'm writing this.

Another "Anesthesia" case writes,

In the past, I have felt unconscious a lot in relationships. I haven't been really there, almost as if I have a certain unreality about my existence, that this is my life *and it's happening to me. I used to feel "remote" from my own life. I have always, in the past, felt I couldn't get what I wanted and felt at the effect of my partner. It seems like I felt my reality more when with someone—needed people or relationship to know I existed—therefore, it was more important to be with anyone than alone.*

This must be from separation from mother after birth, but I also seem to have a hook-up with feeling safe and alive in the center of things—my mother had the rocker, bassinet, changing table, etc. all in a little circle right by her bed, since she wasn't too mobile, and she was with me a lot. I suppress my aliveness and my true self (because I had to be good for my mom). I've always tried to be good instead of going for what I wanted—then resented it and created upsets and separation.

One client, who was breech with anesthesia, reports,

The ways that my birth affects my relationships is that I feel I can't have one, I don't know how to do it right. Even when they are working I have the thought that sooner or later I'll mess them up.

I tend to deaden my aliveness with drugs or with my ego. This keeps me separate from others. I was a very welcome addition to my parents. I set up and create situations—work, family, friends—where I'm always welcome and give lots of approval and love. However, I never allow myself to receive it. Somehow I feel they are only saying these things because they feel sorry for me or are setting me up to hurt me.

My special case (because I was considered a miracle birth) keeps me separate. I feel I'm always right, my way is the best way, and I'm better than others.

Another client reports,

I looked exactly like my father, who immediately expressed his rejection of his self-image. I just realized today that my father wanted a son (hence my own indecision on having a baby—for fear it won't be a girl!). I was taken away from mother and put in a nursery—so I have a fear of abandonment and I always leave a relationship first! Also, I need more holding. My mother was drugged, and I keep recreating opportunities to experience ether/sodium pentathol in surgery. My mother overfed me—I have a weight problem. I was born in early morning. I have an attitude now of attacking the burden of the day each morning when I wake up.

A normal "Anesthesia" birth reports,

I experience struggle in my relationships—especially with my mate. And when the going gets tough, I want to leave; sometimes I leave physically, emotionally, or mentally. Whenever I feel separate, I always feel loss at the same time. I remem-

ber feeling that I had really lost my mother at birth, when in reality we had just been separated. I feel that I need other people to tell me what to do and how to do it. I often feel that I need to get out of a relationship for fear that if I stay I'll get hurt. I often do not feel supported by men because I was delivered by a woman. I have a fear of separation because it makes me feel like I'll lose that person, so sometimes I stay in relationships even when I don't want to go.

A SUMMARY OF DRUGGED AT BIRTH:

(1) Always "in a fog;"
(2) yawn a lot;
(3) fade in and out;
(4) feel "unconscious" in relationships;
(5) complain of "deadening their aliveness" in relationships;
(6) support often equals suffocation in relationships;
(7) complain of finding it hard to focus;
(8) feel ungrounded, disconnected, and smothered;
(9) feel out of touch and disconnected in relationships;
(10) describe having a "spaciness;"
(11) complain of suppressing feelings;
(12) describe themselves as "emotionally cold" in their relationships;
(13) many confess to enjoying drugs in their relationships;
(14) some say they "need to get high" in order to be spontaneous.

AFFIRMATIONS FOR "DRUGGED" BIRTHS:

(1) It's safe to be fully alive!
(2) I no longer need drugs to feel alive.
(3) My aliveness is a pleasure for me and everyone else.
(4) It's easy to be alive.
(5) It's safe to be in my body.
(6) It's safe to feel my feelings.
(7) It's safe to breathe fully and freely.
(8) I now can fear forward.
(9) I forgive my mother for being afraid of childbirth.
(10) I am safe to be with.
(11) It's safe to be intimate.
(12) I can express myself freely and fully.
(13) I no longer have to withhold to survive.
(14) It's safe to be fully out there!

Chapter 16

INDUCED

An induced birth is one in which the labor is artifically started, usually by intravenous drip. Ordinarily, a baby comes when it is ready and begins the process of labor by emitting its own hormone. Sometimes there are "medical reasons" for induction. But sometimes there are less important reasons, even as ridiculous as the parents wanting to have the baby before New Year's to save on taxes, or because the doctor has a golf tournament. Or maybe somebody wanted the baby to be born on some ancestor's birthday. Although it may seem innocent and logical at the time, if those involved knew the effects of this on the baby, we doubt seriously if they would ever try for an induction.

In the beginning of rebirthing, we had almost no inductions in our rebirthing practices. Apparently, induction births had to be "induced" into rebirthing itself! After a few years, they began to show up. Then more and more came, and suddenly we had a whole rash of these types of births.

One of the obvious things is that these people often have trouble "getting started." They may have to be "induced" into new things that they want to do or need to do.

Although they may not be as overtly angry as say a "forceps-type," the anger of an induced person is often more suppressed and covert. They usually resent that their life started on other people's terms. They may *get even* in life for this—by withholding. They may withhold love, withhold sex and affection, or withhold themselves from the world in general: withholding their power, their creativity, their contribution. They may be putting out a vibration like this: "Come and get me. But if you do I will resent it. I will say no to you to prove I can come on my own terms, on my own time." They often keep people waiting, then wonder why people are upset with that.

An induction type of person has not really chosen to be here; somebody else chose, and they, therefore, only half-participate in life. The rebirther must in fact "set up" the induction because of their lack of commitment to being here on earth and to coming out. Possibly they chose to have others start them because they were too frightened to live and get going. If they will face this, they can be healed. If they won't face it, and continue to blame others, they might continue to have problems, especially in relationships.

In a relationship, they may hold back until their mate finally starts pushing them or "inducing" them. Then they will resent it and say "*No.*" This will go around and around, over and over again as the birth script is run and re-run in frustration—until one gets fed up. Sometimes if the recreated "induction" is gentle by the opposite mate, the situation produces good results, and these people become very productive once someone gets them started. However, because the induced person often feels a need to say "no" physically in an attempt to get even, the opposite mate may not be so gentle. He may become the obstetrician in the relationship—even getting pushy and panic—"This baby has to be delivered *now*" type of thing. This makes the induced person balk, retreat, get angrier and withhold more. The severity of this repetitive game often depends on the reason that the induction was done in the first place. If the reason was to "please the parents," the person may have a stronger desire to get even, and the game is "turned up." The attitude becomes "I will do it on *my* terms, *never* on yours." We have run across people that were actually induced to save a few hundred dollars on taxes. This, as you can imagine, often results in tremendous "charge" around money. Some of these people work hard *not* to make money to get even.

Relating to someone who was induced requires a tremendous amount of patience. However, they tend to attract partners who have little or no patience. This can be an unending battle unless both partners are very enlightened and are very willing to release the pattern and help each other.

One can easily see how important this would be in a work situation: The employee may be a very very good worker and just have trouble getting started or showing up on time. If the employer knew something about inductions, he could be more compassionate and not feel like he had to fire the person for just this reason. In a couple situation, it is helpful if both people are up front about it when it is happening and make light of it. "Now I am going to induce you," said in the right tone of voice, can work. It obviously helps most if both people are getting rebirthed.

"Induced births" tend to have problems with commitment—usually their partners have to induce them into choosing a relationship!

One "induction" case reports,

I was induced because the doctor felt I was ready to be born. My mother, who was thirty-seven at the time of my birth, had had a difficult time with my older sister (long labor, forceps, possible death of either mother or child), and she was only twenty months older. Also, I was not planned, and my parents were in a bad financial situation. Possible consequences of these circumstances were a tremendous feeling of guilt—that my being alive meant less for my family. Also, always being compared to my older sister, who resented the hell out of me. I also felt a lot of fear around birth.

I have always had problems with time. I'm always late and pushing and feeling panicky. A major result, I feel, of being induced, is to want a man to do it for me, because I can't get started, but to resent him for pushing me. The feeling of not being wanted for who I am is probably a result of my parents' doubts about having another child, and, I think, disappointment that I wasn't a boy.

One student had to be induced because he was illegitimate and didn't want to come out.

I was prematurely induced at eight months to allow head first delivery as I was turning around persistently in utero. It was a hospital delivery after long-induced labor. I was born near midnight. Also, I was conceived out of wedlock. As a result of all this, I have a strong need to be intimate with women, but also great difficulty due to shyness. I'm afraid of rejection by women. I'm not good enough to be with a woman I desire. I feel helpless in relationships. I do not choose relationships but make the best of what happens if I am in one. I want my partner to serve me in my helplessness. My attitude is often apathetic in relationships. I want to be loved. The main way my birth seems to affect my relationships is that I do not believe I can choose to have an ideal relationship.

Another client writes,

I was induced! They didn't want me to come out too fast. I was the fifth of ten children. Anesthesia! All the rest of the children after me were induced as well. I can't get what I want when I want it is the main theme of my relationships, which seems to stem from my birth. Especially with men; since my OB was a man, he decided when I came out, and, therefore, I let others decide when I come out, whether it be at work, relationships, etc. Resentment sets in! On the other hand, my birth was a miracle between two wonderful saints, and I feel my life has been a miracle.

My father was a very spiritual man who was studying to be a priest before he got married. My mother is a very nurturing, mother-earth type who is always willing to serve. My life is about serving large families with a spiritual mission and desire.

It is also about balancing the two energies within my relationships with men—I still can be spiritual and in physical relationship with a man. My father left the priesthood and married my mom. I am most like my dad and feel that I would have to leave my work to be with a man in a committed relationship. Also, I have lots of relationships around me, both young and old, and I love families. Also, I tend to balance out upsets, people relationships, etc., since I was in the middle of ten children.

The following is an example of a reverse induction, where the baby was induced in order to slow her down.

I was induced because my sister, who is three years older than me, came out early. So I was induced to keep me from being early. My mother was drugged and my father wasn't there. This affects my relationships because the men I want don't want me. I think I need to be drugged to have sex. I feel like men try and stop my growth or swallow my power (like the obstetrician). I'm always early or on time; people have to induce me into a relationship; and nobody ever wants me the way I am.

No wonder this student had such a hard time getting started:

I was induced. There was anesthesia. I was not breastfed. I was separated after birth and put in a nursery. I had a female doctor and I don't think my father was present. Some of the ways this seems to affect my relationships are: I have a hard time starting projects; I lack a male self-image; the anesthesia causes a spacey feeling I have sometimes—I want to go to sleep a lot; I feel I can't get enough—scarcity, and I have a hard time breaking through loving and touching; I think it is due to separation after birth. . . . I also experience intense loneliness at times.

An LRT graduate writes that she was unwanted and therefore had to be induced:

I always feel unwanted, rejected. I jump in first, think later; I fear abandonment; I'm always testing my mate; I think sex equals love; I always want the opposite of my mate to set myself up for rejection. I always hate getting out of bed (the womb), and I dislike change. Also, men seem to play with my affection, then reject me. My mate has to set up the rules and make the commitment, then I feel trapped, like I made a mistake.

A SUMMARY OF INDUCED BIRTHS:

(1) They have a problem "getting started;"
(2) they have a problem with time in general;
(3) they often think that their partner should "do it for them;"
(4) they often feel helpless, waiting for someone to serve them;
(5) there is a tendency not to choose relationships—the partner picked them;
(6) they complain of being apathetic in relationships;
(7) they often have the thought "I can't get what I want;"
(8) people have to induce them to do things, and induce them to be in relationships; then they resent the induction;
(9) often they hate getting out of bed;
(10) they find that "others set up the rules" and then feel trapped in relationships;
(11) in general, there is a hard time starting projects.

AFFIRMATIONS FOR INDUCED BIRTHS:

(1) *It's safe to choose.*
(2) *I forgive people for choosing for me.*
(3) *It's safe to make up my own mind.*
(4) *I no longer need to create others' inducing me.*
(5) *I'm in touch with what I desire.*
(6) *It's safe to express myself.*
(7) *It's safe to assert myself.*
(8) *I forgive myself for waiting, controlling, and blaming*
(9) *I am committed to my own joy and aliveness.*
(10) *I choose life!*
(11) *I'm meant to be here.*
(12) *I'm in charge.*
(13) *I control my own destiny.*
(14) *I'm safe in the hands of God.*
(15) *All my choices support my well-being!*

Chapter 17

BREECH

A breech baby comes out backwards, either "butt first" or else feet first, which is more rare and is called "footling breech." As rebirthers, we study why this person turned around in the womb, since a baby intuitively knows the right way to be delivered. A breech usually turns because he or she was afraid to come out. Often, he sensed some immense problem on the outside, some danger he saw that made him want to *go back*! Or maybe he knew that one or both of his parents wanted a baby of the opposite sex, and he wanted to avoid the disappointment.

Since this kind of birth is obviously harder on the mother, these people grow up with more guilt. They tend to have a fear of hurting people, especially women. In the Loving Relationships Training they express thoughts such as: "I cause pain," "I have to hurt women (or people) in order to survive," "I am guilty!"

Obviously, a breech tends to make things harder in life. He or she tends to turn everything into more of a struggle than it need be. They might even do things backwards. One "footling breech" always put his shoes on the wrong feet and, as an adult, he reports, he feels he always puts his worst foot forward in relationships.

In some cases, the doctor may have attempted to turn this baby manually from the outside in order to get its head down. This is very painful to mother and baby—and definitely adds trauma. Sometimes a cesarian is required.

A breech needs to learn that he can have it easy and survive. A breech needs to learn that it is safe to "come out."

In a relationship, a breech may unconsciously hurt his partner and then feel terribly guilty; but will tend to re-run this pattern as long as he thinks his life depends on it. One of the very first cases we had at the beginning of rebirthing was a man who was quite suicidal. His "presenting complaint" was that he was constantly hurting others and could not stop. And he was so guilty about this he wanted to kill himself. At his birth, when he came out breech, his mother bled a lot and almost died. Therefore, he was terrified to be inside a woman's vagina. Once he was able to connect his suicidal urge to his birth type (which he could not see before rebirthing), a great deal of it just lifted off during the breathing session. The progress he made in just one rebirthing session was astonishing.

A breech needs a lot of release from the thought that he needs to hurt others in order to survive. This addiction to hurting others unconsciously, feeling guilty, punishing oneself for the guilt, then running the whole tape over and over again, is a deep habit glued to the "birth script." The problem is that these births tend to pick partners who have a masochistic desire to be hurt. This reinforces the pattern and the game. Both partners need to acknowledge their role in the game, and, probably, both should be rebirthed, if not with the same rebirther, with two rebirthers who consult with each other.

We had several breeches whose "personal law" (most negative thought about self, usually formed at birth) was: "I am wrong!" They always felt wrong no matter how much we worked with them. Finally, we realized that they were all stuck in the thought that it was wrong to give up the thought "I am wrong!" After that, we finally made some progress.

One student who was breech and induced reports,

The way my birth affects my relationships is I'm always looking for the love to stop coming. I never think it's the right relationship. I always think I do things wrong. I hate getting started. I hate completions. I look for ways to not like the other person. I withhold my exuberance about life. I feel they don't really love me. I feel like there's something strange or wrong with me. I wonder a lot about how I can control the outcome. I never feel satisfied with myself. I never know what's next. I'm always acting like what's given to me is not right. I don't want to speak for myself for fear it will offend someone or be wrong. I try to be amiable when I am emotional.

One young lady writes that she was breech, forceps, and the wrong sex!

*I obviously didn't want to come out into the negative vibrations of their mar-
riage. They had me to "save the relationship" and it never worked. I was very
sensitive to their fighting and tension, and blamed myself. I continue to blame
myself whenever I'm around negative vibrations, so I try to help other people's
hurts, as I tried to heal my parents' marriage. I take responsibility for other people's problems because I feel insecure as a woman (they wanted a boy) and want
to prove my worth and value and desirability. . .and therefore win other people's
love. I tried to win my father's love but it was a struggle. I want to be loved
and desired by everyone—male or female.*

Another young lady, whose birth included conception trauma,
induction, drugs, and finally came out breech, writes,

*. . .so drugs were used to induce it further. It went on for three days. It was very
hard on her. She remembers the doctors or nurses saying finally that I was breech
and she got very upset about that. They eventually put her out with anesthesia,
and I was finally born.*

*She remembers trying to breathe in more and more gas, but they kept taking
it away and keeping her awake until the very end. She was so traumatized she
would not let anyone even drive her by the hospital for over a year after I was
born. They were, however, delighted to have had a girl. . . My parents were al-
coholics and were drunk when I was conceived.*

*A way I think this has affected my relationships is that until the last couple
of years, I never had sex without having had some drinks first. I am also an
alcoholic but have been sober since June, 1981. . . I felt like I was being pulled
out into a vortex—forced out of the womb or pulled out of it unwillingly, and
I have often felt, in my relationships with others, that their will overpowers me.*

*I also have a sense of struggle in relationships. The main way my birth has
affected my relationships is anesthesia—I spent a lot of time being unconscious—I
drift off at odd times, get distracted, or use alcohol to stop immediate pain. But
the use of alcohol just makes the whole problem worse and makes us struggle
longer. Anesthesia at birth has the same effect. It mitigates the immediate pain,
but prolongs and exacerbates the entire process.*

Another breech birth reports the following:

*I was breech. . .labor was very long and painful for both me and my mother.
The ambivalence about leaving the womb carries over into my relationships. I'm
ambivalent about being in the really long term, close ones. . .*

*I felt really lost upon being separated at birth from my mother, and I really
feel devastated when I cannot connect or be in the same general location as my
partner. I don't like being alone for long periods. . . I felt that my slowness at being*

born hurt my mother; hence, I find myself impatient with partner's slower pace when we're together. Although I was loath to leave the womb, I realized on some level that I had to separate to live.

In relationships, I tend to "back out" when there is too much closeness. Because the birth was long and painful, I blamed the male doctor for not "fixing it." I tend to think men aren't really interested in, or sensitive to, women's feelings, especially pain. Men don't really care!

Birth was a struggle, life is a struggle, and relationships are a struggle. Pain follows pleasure, and has since birth. If I experience a lot of pleasure in a relationship, I'll often create an upset to follow. Also, Mother didn't have enough milk, so I wasn't breastfed, so there's never enough! My parents wanted a boy— they already had a daughter, so my thought was, "I'm not good enough." So I try to be better than my partners, or see them as reflections of my not being good enough.

The following was a complicated case—forceps, breech, induced, ten days late, heavy anesthesia:

My mom stained in the third month of pregnancy and almost lost me. Then she fell around the fourth month on the ice. Also, a close cousin died in a parachute accident about a month before I was born. I have a tremendous fear of my own violent death in an airplane crash. . .I come from fear, desperation and survival in relationships. I can't get enough air when I feel anxiety—my own breath is very shallow. I'm frightened of commitment. I'll lose my freedom. I'll have to compromise and not do it my way. I fear marriage a lot—it feels stifling to me. I feel separate from myself—my head from my body (forceps pulling my head off). . .I'm into my head all the time with judgment, and I intellectualize my feelings because I feel separation with myself and others—body numbness. I'm always fighting and struggling to survive!

One of our students, who was a "footling breech," reports:

I tend to go into a relationship, then fight to get out. I'm trapped. I avoid intimacy. I "walk" away when anything stressful happens. I appear open, but my core is closed. I fear abandonment and set up situations to get my partner to leave; then I feel abandoned. I am giving, then I won't let people give back to me; then I get pissed off at being used. I won't let people get close. I'm always testing—I'm unconventional, not restricted, possessive of my own freedom. I'm terrified of rejection; I act cold and superficial. I'm a fighter. I think that the feeling of not being wanted—my mother tried to abort me—makes me terrified of getting close to anyone. I also feel they will consume me; I'll lose my identity. I always feel people are trying to pull me, to force me. I do what they want me *to do, but I also resist everything and everyone. I distance myself to protect myself.*

One young lady started out breech, was manipulated *in utero,* her mother was anesthetized, and then finally she was pulled out with forceps. She writes,

My father was absent during my birth; he was away in the service. My mother felt lost and alone and angry and scared. My mother suspects the doctor did not make it, because she knew he was not in the hospital when I started to arrive. The nurse-nun checked on Mom and discovered I was starting to come out. She screamed, "Stop it! Don't bear down! Hold back! Someone get her into OB!" My mother was then immediately "knocked out."

She says I was breech but manipulated into the correct position, and it was the Head-nurse-nun who actually delivered me. My mother was in a great deal of pain, according to her, and "ripped apart" (her words) during my birth. She felt conflict about the birth, as well as about becoming a mother and her own sexuality in general. When she was six months pregnant, she was involved in an accident, where she was thrown almost out of a car, clung to the door hanging halfway out of the car, the car door swinging against her, hitting her in the stomach repeatedly. . .

As for my relationships, I often feel men aren't there for me, either physically or emotionally, and I have confusion about my own sexuality. I withhold myself in my relationships, only recently learning how to share myself with others with integrity. (I can be who I am, not be someone for someone else.)

I have been very passive in the past, and have created situations where I need to be bailed out or assisted. Then I resent them terribly. I space out, go away, withdraw—emotionally and mentally—when threatened. I don't let go of control, especially in sex—it's difficult to have orgasms, takes a long time; I must feel very secure with whom I'm with. I tend to set it up for people to leave me before I realize I don't want the relationship anymore.

Another woman, who was breech and unwanted, feels guilty for being born:

My feet are not on firm ground, which affects my judgment. Other people try to turn around my thinking. I act before I think. I'm impulsive. I find myself with cold people. I seem to have the need to hurt the people I love. I feel lonely. Being breech led to my feelings of always going in the wrong direction, for which I am always guilty. I must have caused my mother tremendous hurt. Once she had a fall and almost lost me. Maybe I haven't forgiven her for her mistakes and blame her for not taking care of my safety. . .

A SUMMARY OF BREECH BIRTHS:

(1) They complain of "doing things wrong;"

(2) they often hate completion;

(3) they say they "never know what they want next;"

(4) they are afraid of being wrong—this keeps them from speaking up;

(5) complain of "struggle" in relationships;

(6) some say they "back out" of relationships when they get too close;

(7) they notice that pleasure is followed by pain;

(8) they are usually worried about hurting people;

(9) complain of breath being shallow;

(10) there is always fear and desperation to deal with—coupled with a feeling of having a "fight for survival;"

(11) they will go into relationships and then "fight to get out;"

(12) feel an "unconventional possessiveness of freedom;"

(13) complain often of people trying to "pull" and force them;

(14) will often characterize themselves as "fighters;"

(15) complain of not knowing which direction to go;

(16) speak of painful beginnings in life and in relationships;

(17) and, if there was an attempt by the doctor to turn them from the outside, there is then resistance to other people trying to change them—yet at the same time, a daring of others to do so.

AFFIRMATIONS FOR BREECH BIRTHS:

(1) *I forgive myself for thinking I do it wrong.*

(2) *I forgive myself for the pain I think I caused others.*

(3) *My aliveness is safe and pleasurable for me and everyone else.*

(4) *It's safe to have life easy and pleasurable.*

(5) *I can trust pleasure to last.*

(6) *I forgive myself for perceiving others as "out to get me."*

(7) *People support me in having my freedom.*

(8) *People add to my safety.*

(9) *People now support me in an easy and pleasurable manner.*

(10) *I am completely innocent.*

(11) *I can now get off to a good start.*

(12) *It's safe and fun to start over.*

(13) *My passion for peace gets me what I want.*

(14) *Since I'm a winner, it's easy for me to succeed.*

(15) *I'm always free to come and go as I please.*

(16) *Since I'm free, I'm comfortable.*

(17) *All my relationships make my life easier and more pleasurable.*

(18) *My way is the right way.*

(19) *I can take any turn I choose.*

(20) *It's safe to go my own way.*

(21) *I can make it any way I choose.*

(22) *I can survive without fighting.*

Chapter 18

FORCEPS

Babies born with the "help" of forceps had their heads scrunched, screwed, twisted, and pulled out of the womb. The rest of the body came along for the ride. Imagine being a tooth pulled out of your own mouth, and you'll get the idea.

Forceps babies often develop migraine headaches as adults, and, even worse, life itself can become one huge headache for them. Sometimes, especially during rebirthing sessions, you can actually see the impression of the forceps on their temples. These might be scrappy, feisty kids, spunky street-fighters, full of life and the desire to do things their own way. They are often very intuitive, creative, and independent. They don't trust support—can you blame them?—which, in their minds, equals having their heads handed to them. (Perhaps John the Baptist was a forceps delivery?) "No, thank you," is often their response to people who offer assistance. They'd prefer to go at life alone, headstrong and tenacious!

Why does a baby need forceps? Because it is too big, too slow, too twisted, too far down the canal for a c-section—whatever the reason, it is stuck, and the obstetrician sees his role as the liberator. Later in life, forceps babies tend to create the same pattern of getting stuck, then attracting someone to bail them out at the last minute. This can turn out to be an enormous asset in life, once the trauma of the first bail-out is released.

We know a great deal about "forceps relationships" because Bob's wife, Mallie, was born such, though at home rather than in a hospital. A forceps case tends to give double messages in relationships—on the one hand, communicating she can do it herself, she doesn't need you, get out of her way, her way is better. . .an attitude based on the desire to prove she didn't really need the forceps in the first place. And, on the other hand, two of her primal thoughts tend to be: "No matter how much I do, it's not enough," and "I need help in the end." So she tends to imply neediness, covertly and at the last minute.

We can think of times Mallie was driving the car. It was time to make a left turn and she would say, "We make a left here, don't we?" The tag line, "don't we?" is the key to the forceps. You see, Mallie knows the right way to go, but she suggests that she might need correction, while, at the same time, coming from the authority of being in the driver's seat.

The best thing to do with forceps people is to support them gently in following through on choices they make for themselves. Don't be too helpful, however, or they'll think you're out to get them. And don't be too pushy or it will activate old wounds. Since forceps are extremely painful to the newly born, soft-skulled baby, even the slightest rememberance of this experience is intolerable, even to a fully grown adult. Seeing a crane on the street or tongs in a kitchen could suddenly awaken this memory.

Since a forceps type is often terrified of being manipulated by others, he will be obsessed with being in control, playing the obstetrician rather than the innocent victim, turning the tables on his birth scenario, gaining the upper hand. In Bob's relationship with Mallie, letting go of control and allowing divine guidance to show the way has been a constant motif. Bob remembers one time when he suggested she take a "helpless day." She works so hard and so well, it seemed it would be a wonderful gift if she took a full day off and let Bob serve her while she lay in bed all day. She grew suspicious! What was his ulterior motive? And she only surrendered when he would agree to follow her directions—so it became a controlled helpless day.

One forceps baby remembers they called him a "metal head." His delivery was quick (one hour), and his mother was anesthetized. He reports,

In most of my relationships I create a lot of struggle. Also, my "big head" created lots of rips and tears in relationships, i.e. I over-intellectualize and distance myself by analyzing myself and others excessively. I am afraid of creating pain in others, and, therefore, have had difficulty saying no to women. My ego is very tied up with my head and very defensive at the same time.

Around the time of my birth, my father was enraged at someone and hit him, breaking his right fist. Forty years later, my right fist was operated on for arthritic deterioration. . .My anticipation of pain was so acute that I recreated it in my arthritis and in the pain of difficult relationships. . .I often get people to pull me out of tough situations.

Another forceps child recalls that his neck was crooked and he was dropped by the doctors:

I feel that my birth made me feel the world was an ugly, painful place, and that people generally are incompetent. I've also always felt very separate from my body, very mental. I've never much enjoyed being touched. I don't like massages. Since my obstetrician was a stiff, authoritarian German, I don't like authority figures and have never gotten along with them. However, since I had to be helped along with forceps, I feel I need help in getting started with anything. Actually, I have too much dependency and need, and resist help. I hate being manipulated or pushed in any way. . .Since I was conceived in rape and born in Nazi Germany, I feel the world is crazy, illusory, and dangerous. I have never felt I really wanted to be here. This is always connected with a sense that God has forsaken me. I have never ever felt responsible or that I could be responsible for my life.

Another man, who was very big and stuck in the birth canal, reports that his mother had an episiotomy at his birth. He came out with the help of forceps, then grew up to become a Rolfer. He writes,

My birth was somewhat difficult because I was a large baby. I was stuck in the canal—my shoulder was caught. So forceps were used. As a result, I get angry when men interfere in my relationships. I struggled a lot, and in the past I certainly acted that out in my relationships, especially the intimate ones. I sometimes confuse support with attack, help with injury. Perhaps the main thought I have is that to be successful in relationships I have to leave. It's a lose/lose situation—either my relationships have been filled with struggle and anger, or I leave them behind, thinking that to be a successful completion. Sometimes that has been true, but often has not. Thank God that's all changing.

One young lady shares her birth script:

My mother's water breaks; I thought I wasn't ready, very angry, tried to leave and couldn't—stuck in body, angry, then frightened, frozen stuck, then pulled

out with forceps. . . .

The results in my relations are that the men I think I need to survive are the ones I fear will destroy me. Men hurt me. People in general hurt me accidentally. I often don't feel ready for the next step in relationships. I feel terror, trapped. I have to leave. I'm angry about separation, particularly in friendships. My mother didn't want me to leave her. I have an aversion to touch, sometimes a heightened enjoyment of touch also.

Another such case writes,

I am afraid of touch because "touch equals pain," yet I feel a real need for comforting and tenderness and being held—conflict! I always have to leave a relationship to find freedom; therefore, I sabotage it at some point. I don't trust myself, my own feelings, my intuition.

One man took three days to get out:

I had a tremendous struggle to get out. My mother was drugged and couldn't help. I made a decision, "Women aren't there for me." They wouldn't support me. I had to do it all myself. As a result, I've created women in my life who weren't there for me and wouldn't support me. The ones who were, I couldn't accept. . .I had to get out to survive. So I was always thinking about leaving. I've also spent a lot of time being unconscious in my relationships. . .I also have feelings that I can't do it myself. I need someone to pull me out.

A SUMMARY OF FORCEPS BIRTHS:

(1) They dislike being controlled and manipulated;
(2) they are more comfortable being in control;
(3) they fear pain and think pleasure leads to be pain;
(4) they often feel pulled out of situations;
(5) they think they have to do it all themselves;
(6) they think that no matter how much they do, it's not enough;
(7) they fear they can't make it on their own;
(8) they feel not good enough, unworthy, or that something's wrong with them;
(9) they feel that their heads and their hearts are separate, i.e., disconnected from their feelings;
(10) they often fear touch.

AFFIRMATIONS FOR FORCEPS BIRTHS:

(1) I forgive my obstetrician completely.

(2) I can do it on my own!

(3) I know how to make it.

(4) I'm good enough to make it.

(5) I do enough to make it easily.

(6) I always find endings easy and pleasurable.

(7) Since I can do it on my own, it's safe to let others help.

(8) I now experience all support as self-support.

(9) I can relax and let others do the hard work.

(10) I can now see that people who want to support me want to pleasure me and make life easier.

(11) The more I relax and take it easy, the more I experience support as pleasure.

(12) I no longer fight support.

(13) It's a pleasure to have others do it for me.

(14) My innocence generates pleasurable support.

(15) I am heading for more ease and pleasure.

(16) My head leads the way to pleasure.

(17) My heart safeguards my head no matter what!

Chapter 19

CORD AROUND NECK

As you can guess, they hate to wear ties!

A baby can become entangled in the cord in a variety of ways, and oftimes the entanglement is loose and easily corrected. But if the cord is pulled tight around the neck, then the very source of survival becomes an instrument of strangulation. This creates a primal schizophrenia towards life; these children often grow up to have a love/hate relationship with life. Life and death become entwined in their consciousness. When things get too exciting, they will scream, "This is killing me!" They will get all choked up over things, holding their fear in their throat like a lump they can't swallow. You can hear the "stuckness" in their voices—it can sound like a telephone operator whose vocal cords and sinuses have switched places.

Since life threatened them so much at birth, they often have a need to create life-threatening situations in later life in order to feel their aliveness. They are masters of making mountains out of mole hills.

These people may be "cut off" from feelings below the neck. They feel, but not nearly as much as they could or should. In relationships, they have a push/pull time of it. On the one hand, they tend to crave umbilical attachments. On the other hand, they push their partners away. They get entangled in love, as though it were the cord itself, then try to extricate themselves. Again, if your partner had this type of birth, you might get set up as the obstetrician, and you may be looked upon as the controller, manipulator, life threatening savior not to be trusted. The best approach here is to be strong, loving, relaxed, and consistent. Any double messages could drive your partner nuts.

If you were born with the cord around your neck, you may find your relationships "sticky." Intimacy might be tricky. The closer someone gets to you, the more he loves you, the more you may be reminded of the close call at birth, when getting free of the cord was essential for your survival. The issue of freedom and commitment may be especially complicated for you.

One client reports,

I don't remember too much of my birth. Mom died before I could ask her and Dad wasn't there—but in rebirths I have gotten in touch with a fairly long and slow struggle, then coming in in a rush and almost strangling myself on my cord. I think my mother was anesthetized; I also believe I was separated from her quickly. It was a hospital birth.

In my relationships, I always had the need to cling to men, for fear they would leave—at the same time wanting space and pushing them away. Fear of closeness—as too overwhelming—means I can't totally be in love and be permanent. So I want out. There always has been a fear of loss, death, and separation—mainly with men and never with women (my mother was always there for me during the first few years of my life).

I also have a strong belief that my self-expression could be strangled—smothered—if I stayed in a close relationship.

Another student of ours shares,

One of my basic feelings is that of being a loser. I'm a terrible competitor, and when I near the end of something, I surrender and give up. There is a feeling of worthlessness. I'm afraid to get close. One-to-one relationships cause strangulation. I cannot give fully.

My relationship to clothes as a kid was: I remember always begging my mother—don't button my top button, or I can't wear a tie. If something touched my neck, I gagged.

I find myself lagging behind. I have to do things at my own pace to feel safe. Or I'll do crazy things where there is danger. I like danger and chance.

I've always felt my life is to be spent alone though I don't want it to be that way. In the past I've been in trouble with the law a few times.

An LRT graduate recalls,

Significant factors of my birth were: The cord was wrapped around my neck twice; I was a blue baby; I was very big. My mother thought I was dead while she was carrying me. The doctor thought I was dead at one point during the delivery. I had so much anesthesia that my mother was afraid I wouldn't open my eyes for the photograph that was taken two days later.

How my birth affects my relationships is: I used to numb myself with a lot of alcohol; I feel too big, and so I chose a job where I used to have to weigh in every six months; I feel relationships with men are suffocating and used to have a very clear exit from the relationship from the very beginning; I used to enjoy high drama and found life and death situations attractive; I feel I can't breathe in a relationship.

Another such case suggests,

One way in which my birth affects my relationships is that I feel trapped; too much closeness brings up fear. Anger is a mask that pushes love away so that I don't have to feel afraid. My dream-memory of the cord around my neck is warm and sensual, leading to an experience of ecstasy and aliveness. Maybe the drugs took away my fear, drugs lead to altered states—out-of-the-body experiences and ultimately union. Fortunately, my drug experience led me (or seemed to) to God—the inner self—so I don't want or need drugs, but I do feel one with God. I have not made "conscious" choices in relationships—only choices from my "patterns." Somehow being "a girl" is associated with fear of pregnancy.

One student confesses,

My birth has affected my relationships in that I'm cold and rigid (turning purple represents this). When the air was cut off at my birth, I feel it affected the way I don't communicate my emotions/feelings. I'm not open enough. I always have to be in control; maybe I felt like I didn't have control when the cord was around my neck! I always feel like I have to be strong and healthy, can't show any weakness; if I show weakness, then I will be helpless, and I will need others' help—I can't do that!

This case was premature, forceps, cord wrapped around her neck, heart stopped—she had to be revived:

I feel very alone. It has been hard for me to allow others into my life. I can't allow them in unless they give me unconditional love right up front. Consequently, I have had very few close relationships, friendships, or loves. If people saw good in me, I was sure they were wrong. My own mother could see no good in me, and Mother is always right! I knew that these thoughts were out of balance, *and I began working on them after my first marriage failed.*

The main reason my birth process affects my relationships: I live every day as though I will be rejected and left. As long as I know it could happen, and I live in anticipation of it, it will not suprise me, and so I am prepared! My parents had problems as married people. How they ever got together is a mystery to me!

Fortunately, I have met and married a loving, supportive man, and I am in the process of convincing myself that I deserve to be loved and that I am lovable.

SUMMARY OF CORD AROUND NECK BIRTHS:

(1) They tend to create life-threatening situations;
(2) they are very sensitive to feelings of being "choked;"
(3) intimacy can be risky business;
(4) often, they don't like ties or their top button closed;
(5) they often feel strangled in relationships;
(6) they do well in crisis situations;
(7) they often feel cut off from their emotions;
(8) they often say, "this is killing me," when they feel most alive;
(9) any kind of entanglement can represent primal panic;
(10) they tend to sabotage creations—"killing off" creativity.

SOME AFFIRMATIONS THAT MIGHT HELP:

(1) I can breathe freely and fully, even when things get tense.
(2) Life is safe and easy!
(3) I am free.
(4) It's safe to be intimate!
(5) I no longer need to create crises in order to prove I can make it.
(6) I can live without death.
(7) I no longer need entanglements in order to feel alive.
(8) All my relationships loosen me up.
(9) I am loose in love.
(10) I can express all my feelings freely and easily.
(11) I can let go and live.

(12) It's safe to be out of control.

(13) When I surrender, I'm free.

(14) My creations thrive. I allow them to grow and be healthy.

Chapter 20

TWINS

Twins can be more psychic and telepathic because they develop an intuitive connection in the womb. Recent studies have proven that even twins who are separated at birth will grow up with remarkable similarities, including the names of their wives, children, dogs and cats, as well as their careers, hobbies, and interests.

It has always been amazing to us to be involved in rebirthing twins. Usually while rebirthing the one, the other would also get rebirthed spontaneously—even when the second one lived thousands of miles away and didn't know the first was getting rebirthed. We would often get reports like this after rebirthing a twin. "My twin in Europe called me last night and asked 'what were you doing yesterday? I could not stop crying around 3 PM. I could not stop thinking about our mother. I was feeling very separate. . .'"

On some occasions we have had the opportunity to rebirth twins together. It all depends on their relationship. (It is almost imperative to point out that when you rebirth one twin, you are on some level rebirthing the other even if the other is not present. Therefore, the ethical thing to do is to discuss this openly and decide how to handle it.)

Usually, the twin who came out first has some guilt. And usually, the twin who came out second has some anger and feeling of being left. There is often quite a bit of separation trauma going on.

In the case where the mother and/or doctor did not know there was a second twin, that one usually has the thought "Nobody notices me," or, "I am an afterthought," or, "I shouldn't be here."

The most traumatic situation is if there is a dead twin and the other survives. . .especially if the dead twin remains *in utero* for a while. The twin that then survives usually ends up with the thought, "In order for me to survive, someone else has to die." These people often attract deaths in their lives, and then they feel responsible. In one case a soldier we knew survived in Viet Nam, yet many of his buddies died. He kept attributing that to mistakes *he* made in the war, then blamed himself and was devastated. (He had had a dead twin in the womb.) In another extreme case, a woman had a dead twin and her father buried it in the back yard. She grew up playing over her dead twin. She felt she survived because her twin died. Her son, who was a friend of ours, ended up with the thought, "I need to be dead in order for others to survive." He adopted this bizarre thought because of his mother's subconscious thought: "In order for me to survive, somebody has to be dead." Our friend was unconsciously trying to die to satisfy his mother's mind. It took us years to figure out this case. We didn't get it until we actually went to meet his mother and interviewed her about *her* birth and studied family albums.

If twins have a good relationship throughout, then they can become very high and very clear, because they constantly have a "mirror" to see themselves in the other twin. They should be helped to take advantage of this.

Sometimes twins have the thoughts "I am separate," "There is no room for me," "I'm incomplete," or "I need someone else to be whole." Often, they have an intense need for private space.

The following is a report from a set of twins. The first one out shares,

I've always been a leader. I was born first and my twin sister became my first follower. It was very natural for me to be her "big brother" even though I was only fifteen minutes ahead of her at birth. The doctor said she was eager to catch up to me. All our life, my sister and I have had this type of relationship—whenever I do something, like go to Europe, write poetry, take piano lessons, my sister does the same thing shortly afterwards.

When I got married, my sister got married exactly fifteen weeks later. My sister had her first child fifteen days after my wife delivered. And so forth and so on.

I have this same type of relationship with women. My wife always wants to do what I do, go where I go, and achieve what I achieve. We met in college and were both studying philosophy. We were very competitive. My grades were al-

ways just a little higher than hers. I felt guilty for being ahead of her and switched majors—to psychology. So did she. The pattern continued of my being slightly better than her.

When we go skiing or play tennis, this fierce pattern of competition comes up again. I'm sure that at my birth it was a race to the finish whether my sister or I would lead the way. I won that race but have been paying the price ever since.

The second one out summarizes his perspective:

My brother came out first. He clearly led the way. Even though he was only a few minutes ahead of me, he was always referred to as my older brother. He always seemed to have some unspoken advantage over me. I could never be as good as him, with girls, with sports, with school, and later with money.

In my relationships I tend to play second fiddle. I expect women to lead the way for me, show me how to do things. I feel hopeless about succeeding. I'm wonderful at supporting a woman, but whenever a woman supports me in being out in the world more, I feel angry, pushed, and controlled. It feels unnatural to think of myself first. I always take others into consideration. In sex I make sure my partner comes first (am I making love to my twin brother in every woman?). My life seems to stay on the back burner while the women I'm with grow rapidly, then eventually leave me.

I've never made it financially. When I'm really down and out, I usually call my twin brother and he bails me out. I guess I've been hopelessly second best, second string, second fiddle. Now that I know why, I intend to start thinking of myself as number one a little more.

Another second born twin says he was unwanted,

The main ways my birth focuses on my relationship is that I am always feeling unwanted in relationship. I don't feel much aliveness (much sadness), and I'm constantly obsessed and freaked out with being left by my partner.

Also, there is always a sense of not wanting to take responsibility for myself, blaming my partner, and being taken care of by twin (extreme dependence).

I tend to be extremely lazy and just want to lie around and make love, but I don't have much energy to complete things.

SUMMARY OF TWIN BIRTHS:

(1) The first twin is often a leader;
(2) the second twin is often a follower;
(3) they feel that others have advantages over them;
(4) complain of playing "second fiddle" in relationships;

(5) often expect their partner to lead the way;

(6) find it unnatural to think of self first;

(7) in sex, they make sure that their partner finishes first;

(8) feel that they've always been on the "back burner;"

(9) their partners often grow rapidly and then leave;

(10) complain of extreme dependence;

(11) they also tend to be very intuitive, psychic;

(12) want their own space;

(13) feel extreme sibling rivalry and competition;

(14) have a terrible fear of closeness, intimacy, but crave it.

AFFIRMATIONS FOR TWINS:

(1) *It's safe to share my space.*

(2) *I forgive myself for being number one (for first born).*

(3) *I deserve to be number one (for second born).*

(4) *I am innocent.*

(5) *It's safe to be intimate.*

(6) *I am whole and complete.*

(7) *I am innocent no matter what!*

(8) *I can survive without another.*

(9) *I am one of a kind.*

(10) *I have a unique purpose to fulfill.*

(11) *I am a natural leader.*

(12) *I no longer have to follow to survive (for second born).*

(13) *I am enough!*

(14) *I have all the space I need.*

IV

PERINATAL
INFLUENCES

Chapter 21

SEPARATION ANXIETY

We remember rebirthing a very powerful man who literally cried for three hours when he re-experienced the memory of being separated from his mother immediately after his birth. Going through this release changed his life, and obviously his relationship with women. We remember crying *with* him over this and just holding him. Although that was a quite extreme case, how do we know that most people can't have that much sadness around this issue? Maybe he just had the ability to let it all out, all at once.

In the book *Birth Without Violence*, Dr. LeBoyer states that we have "unlimited sadness" about the way we were mistreated at birth. And one of the things people are definitely sad about is the fact that we were taken from our mothers too soon. We wanted to stay next to her, to be bonded, to be held and given "TLC" and the breast. "Rooming-In" was an improvement over being rushed away to a nursery. However, we don't think Rooming-In is even as great as what we saw in Bali: in Bali, the new babies are held next to the parents' bodies for six months. They are not allowed to touch the ground at all. In the sixth month, there is a religious ceremony called a "grounding ceremony," where the baby is first put down. As a result of this practice, the children are exceptionally good, have tremendous self-esteem and security, and grow up to be strong and independent adults.

What are the effects on a person of being separated immediately from his mother at birth? In rebirthing, we have seen how much separation produces deep traumatic scars. It is obvious, we think, to see that all this could lead to feelings of deprivation and worthlessness. The infant is suddenly expelled from its paradise into a world of separation—the first separation being from the mother's body itself, the second separation being taken farther away into a different room, the nursery. All of this separation reminds the being of its original separation—thinking we were separated from God at conception.

You add up all this separation, and the baby's thought becomes "In order to survive, I have to be separate." This decision makes a person feel alone and in fear and guilt the rest of his life. Even if he is with a mate, as long as that thought is still embedded in a person, he will probably have trouble in relationships. Either he will not find one, or if he does, he will slowly push that person he loves away, so he can again become separate.

So, life often becomes this: "Because I am separate from God, I have to deal with this searing pain of my own nothingness by finding someone to join with. But I have trouble finding someone to join with because I am stuck in remaining separate in order to survive. If I do happen to suppress that thought long enough in order to let in a mate, I will have to slowly get rid of him in order to be separate again, or else I will be separate from him even though I am under the same roof with him. I feel miserable and sad because of this, and that makes me even more separate, because nobody wants to be with someone who is miserable and sad. Therefore, I will separate myself from life (die)."

Other decisions babies make as a result of this separation are: "I cannot get my needs met." And, of course, since thoughts create results, this person grows up not getting what he wants. Whatever you believe to be true, you create. The more someone does not get what he wants, the less he believes he *can* get what he wants, and the less he *will* get what he wants. Therefore, he becomes angry and feels ripped off. He is likely to project this anger onto the world and onto his body. Then, of course, he cannot get what he wants in relationships either, so he is likely to end up with the thought "Nothing works for me," and eventually it all feels hopeless.

Many people we have rebirthed who were recalling the separation switch (post-partum) also made the decision: "There is something wrong with me" (why else would they take me away from my mother?); or, "I must have done something bad in order to be stuck away by myself." These beings grow up thinking they actually do have *something* wrong with them. That thought actually *creates* something wrong with them. We have been amazed at how many people we have processed who have symptoms in the body that were a result of the birth thought, "There is something wrong with me."

With the thought "I must be bad," the person will tend to keep punishing himself the rest of his life. Or, if the thought was, "I am worthless," then this person has a very hard time in life and suffers from low self-esteem and an inability to succeed.

In summary, some of the thoughts that babies form as a result of post-partum-separation are:

"I have to be alone and separate in order to survive"
"They don't want me"
"I must have done something wrong"
"I must be worthless"
"I can't get what I want"
"My needs will never be met"
"Love is outside of me and I can't get it"
"I am terrified"

This traumatic experience of separation leaves us feeling vulnerable and inadequate. No wonder Otto Rank placed great emphasis, in his early work, on the significance of the birth trauma in the etiology of all neurosis!

From then on, we must learn to cope with the harsh realities of a separated life in a world experienced as hostile and threatening. This all-pervasive sense of separation, alienation, isolation, and helplessness remains with us. We were somehow wrong. . .(or else we wouldn't have been mistreated this way); and since we were "wrong," we are guilty; and since we are guilty, we must be punished; since we deserve punishment, it is sure to come and, therefore, we must live in fear.

These are just some of the ramifications we have seen in our work involving the separation around birth.

It is our responsibility to change birth practices to prevent this kind of atrocity in future generations. Meanwhile, what is the healing for those who have tremendous separation anxiety embedded within as a result of their birth?

Start by correcting the thought "I am separate from

God." Adopt the thought "I am one with God." As soon as you realize that, God can help you. That is the beginning of changing everything.

Read *A Course in Miracles*. This will help tremendously to heal all separation.

Get rebirthed (see back).

Try the following affirmations: "I forgive everyone at birth for separating me from my mother," or "The more I let myself be joined with others and with love, the more alive I am."

Take the seminars that will help heal this situation (see back).

Pray to be released from all separation.

Chapter 22

FINANCIAL WOES

We have rebirthed many people who were conceived and born during the depression. They obviously formed a lot of thoughts about that, and you can easily imagine what they might be: thoughts like, "I am a burden," "I am a financial burden," "I cause difficulty," "Life is difficult," "It is hopeless," etc.

On a smaller scale, what about a baby born into a family who has financial woes, even if the nation is prospering and the times are good? To the baby, the parent's reality *is* the whole world while they are in the womb. So the results (adopted thoughts) are the same. These people end up being convinced they are a burden. In later life, they feel like a financial burden to their mates. They are using up so much effort wrestling with that thought all the time that they have very little energy left to produce, and often they don't make as much money as they are capable of.

Ideally, before conception, parents should have sensible financial planning. A baby should be conceived *consciously*; when the parents feel that they can handle it financially. If a baby *is* born in a situation where there is potential financial strain, the parents should maintain positive thoughts and send them to the baby. "There will be enough for you." "We welcome you and the joy and love you will bring get us so high that we will attract more money." "The blessings you bring us with your life itself improve our prosperity consciousness." These affirmations are more than important. They are crucial if you want to alleviate guilt. These thoughts will actually attract more money. Having limited thoughts won't. There are many seminars and books one can read to increase prosperity consciousness.

We have rebirthed several people who were actually "induced" around the Christmas-New Year's holiday in order to save money on taxes. This tends to produce a lot of resentment, to put it mildly. Inductions usually have resentment anyway—that "somebody else decided when they should come." If they were induced for mere money reasons, they find that to be even more intolerable and often are even more resentful. They may "get even" by not producing well financially in the world, even though they have tremendous potential and talent.

A family can instill an atmosphere of *abundance* into the mind of a new being *even if* they are a fairly low income family. For example, Sondra's father had a serious illness and could not work a lot of the time, and the family had tremendous medical bills beyond what the insurance would pay. Her mother's salary as a teacher wasn't that much. However, they always had the feeling of abundance, and that there was enough, because her parents were always growing gardens, plants, trees, and farm animals, and they always kept an abundance of food in the house. Mother made clothes, so there was plenty of that, too. Mostly, they did not verbally complain, nor ever once imply that Sondra's new presence cost them too much.

We remember the story about a family who turned three boys into millionaires, even though the parents had little money. One of the things the parents did was keep a fish bowl full of dollars and cash on the piano. The boys were allowed to take out of it the money they wanted; they only had to leave a slip of paper in the bowl stating how much they took out and for what purpose. The parents always made sure there was some money in there. The boys got the thought early: "There is *always* plenty of money for me."

One must be careful to clear all negative thoughts about money before pregnancy. Up to this time we have been talking about thoughts that were *verbalized*. However, the *unverbalized* thoughts of the parents about money can convey to the child a "poor" attitude even before birth.

We have heard other unfortunate stories from clients where right before the birth itself, the father was complaining about the hospital fees for the delivery. That is not exactly the kind of thing a new baby, about to come out, should have to be subjected to. The baby can hear it all, feel it all. The baby knows every worry the mother and father have, every complaint, every thought and fear.

In closing we'd like to say that: one nice idea would be to bring the baby presents of money during the baby showers and the pregnancy in general. At the time of birth, the baby should receive banks and gifts of money. Money will be natural to it.

Chapter 23

EARLY NOURISHMENT

It's not how you're fed as an infant that ultimately affects you; it's the thoughts about how you're fed.

If your mother is guilty about not breast feeding you, that guilt could create upset for you. On the other hand, if your mother has a strong need to be needed, and will not wean you when you're ready, you may conclude that it's not okay to grow up and be independent—that somehow your independence is a threat to your mom. If she thinks there's not enough, you could inherit this thought. If she feels you are hurting her when she breastfeeds you, this could add to your primal guilt, and, indeed, turn into guilt around food, money, love, etc.

If your mom thinks something's wrong with her for not being able to breastfeed you right, you may buy into that thought. The point here is that, since thoughts are creative, it's what was thought, more than what actually happened, that continues to affect you now.

One of the interesting things we began to research in rebirthing was what we called the "Undernourishment Syndrome," due to lack of breast feeding, allergy to formula, or "scheduled feeding." This often resulted in the thought: "I can't get enough" (milk). This was later translated into: "I can't get enough money." The more a person breathed out and changed his thoughts about lack, the more his prosperity increased!

We think it is also obvious that early nourishment problems affect one's relationship to food. This is so obvious that we hardly have to mention it. But it is always surprising to us just how many are *not* breast fed, and how many had to put up with forced feedings.

I (Sondra) had the following experience in this area:

I was one of those babies that was not breast fed, even though I was born at home. In my case, my mother was told *not* to breast feed me because she had some kind of cyst left over from breast feeding my sister. This was a source of great sorrow both to my mother and to myself. I felt ripped off, and so did she. I never had a good relationship with food or with money, or with my sister, until recently, when I finally got clear on all of this.

A rebirther once gave me an assignment to help me clear my "undernourishment trauma." He suggested that I go on a milk diet for seven days. I had tremendous resistance to this assignment. A year went by. I kept *thinking* about it, but did not do it. I kept "working up to it." Finally, I "worked up to it" on my way to do a training in New York City. I decided to fast on milk during the Loving Relationships Training, since I often fasted on juice only during the LRT anyway. So, I checked into the hotel and strolled down to the restaurant, asking the waiter to bring me a glass of milk. He looked at me shocked: "But Madam," he said, "don't you know there is a *milk strike* in New York? . . .there is no milk anywhere!" I suddenly became furious—very unusual for me. I almost never get angry. I was surprised at my sudden reaction. And then, *I had to laugh!* How perfect! I had to set it up perfect. I couldn't get *any* milk—I couldn't get the breast. I suddenly got in touch with *all* of those feelings. I felt deprived. I felt sad. I went "through it."

One week later, in San Diego, I actually started the milk diet. I don't even like milk that much, but I did it. Once, I cheated and had chocolate milk. Another time I had a few spoons of ice cream. . .but mostly I stuck to it for seven days. About the third day, I started feeling like lying on the floor, curled up in the fetal position. I kept breathing—rebirthing myself in this position. The fourth and fifth day, I put a blanket over me and stayed curled up like that for longer periods. The sixth day, I really started experiencing infancy feelings, and, to my delight, I got into the *"sweetness of life."* This was a real healing, and I kept on forgiving.

Then on the last day, a wonderful Dutch rebirther named Hans dropped by, and I told him what I was doing. He said, "Well, since you were not breast fed, this calls for a bottle." He actually went out and got me a bottle, filled it with milk, and proceeded to hold me in his lap and bottle feed me. I became really angry again at the rubber tip (my first feeding was awful, to me). I did not like it at all. I went through the last part of my "trauma;" I breathed it out. It worked. This process worked.

One of the thoughts that I formed around all this as an infant was, "I can't get what I want" (food, the breast, enough). Another thought I formed at birth about this was, "My mother can't give me what I want." And yet another was, "I hate my sister for causing this." These thoughts constantly affected my relationships. If I ever had a man set up as my mother, I could never get what I wanted from him. I felt he never gave to me. I couldn't receive, either, because I was not used to getting. But I made the mistake of resenting men instead of seeing that it was my own case. I never did feel close to my sister. We had a very distant relationship, it seemed to me. I used to ask her for things she did not want to lend to me, which just proved I could create a further case against her. Later, after the "milk diet," I wrote and apologized to her about all this. It was not until then that I began to understand why our relationship has been strained.

Since my first feeding was uncomfortable, I formed some uncomfortable thoughts about food: "Food interrupts my bliss;" "Food is an invasion;" "Other people make me do food their way and I resent it." In general, I never had a good relationship with food. (This of course, was partly due to the fact that I was born on the kitchen table.)

So, that is my own story. What healed me was: the milk diet; rebirthing; writing the book *The Only Diet There Is*; and dining with people who have mastered fine cuisine. I also got help from my spiritual teachers.

There can be, of course, other nourishment traumas besides lack of breast feeding. Maybe you were breast fed, but your mother was not happy or enjoying it while she was doing it. In that case, getting the milk easily could be difficult, and perhaps it did not taste right, and perhaps you felt your mother's tension, and it produced tension in you. If "Mother is anxious" during breast feeding, this will produce "provoking hormones" which often cause colic. Colic (sharp pains in the stomach) makes the baby's abdomen distended, creates gas in the rectum, and stiffening of the legs—all of which often produce piercing screams. There is more to learn about it, but if you had frequent colic, it may have made your mother even more irritable. What "went down" in the relationship with you and your parents during these periods was likely to be rather unpleasant.

Write down all your thoughts about nourishment:

Example:

"Nourishment is difficult."
"Nourishment is a problem."
"Nourishment is no fun."
"I am not in charge of my own nourishment."

We have discovered a definite correlation between early nourishment patterns and the way one receives love and/or money as an adult.

I (Bob) had the following experience in this area:

I was fed on a schedule. Just what the doctor ordered! "Feed him every four hours no matter what!" That's just what my mother did. I would cry and cry and scream and howl. I was hungry! It made no difference. I had to wait my four hours. By the time my mom would try to feed me I was so furious I would spit the food in her face.

I had the thought: "I can't get what I want when I want it." It seemed that everything in my life—food, money, love—was dependent on other people's convenience, their schedules. As I grew up, I rejected my mother's food, and love, more and more. She'd make me sandwiches to take to school. I'd throw them out.

Meal time was always crisis time in my house, and my impossible demands made it all the more insane. I remember my mother running around preparing three different meals for my dad, sister, and myself—no matter how much she did, it was never enough.

When I grew up and moved out on my own, this pattern continued with all my women. We'd fight at dinner time, and I somehow felt un-nurtured in my relationships.

Financially, I carried this pattern to its extreme. It seemed I could never make money except when other people let me have some. Paychecks became the schedule of my survival. I could never source my own businesses. Self-employment equalled unemployment for me. Finally, I affirmed the thought, "I can always get what I want when I want it!"

Gradually, I began to reverse the pattern. I rebirthed, sucking juice from a baby bottle. I got to feel and release all the anxiety and anger around the way I was fed as an infant. I forgave my mother for listening to the doctor. I forgave the doctor for his ignorant advice. A child should be fed according to his natural rhythm of eating, not according to some arbitrary feeding hours, as though he were an animal in the zoo—for that matter, why do we feed animals in the zoo on a schedule? Isn't it unnatural?

The more I forgave and re-claimed myself as the source of my nourishment, the more my mealtimes became a time of ease and pleasure, the more my financial woes disappeared and the more my love life produced a steady flow of nurturing for me.

Chapter 24

NAMING THE CHILD

Although it is common sense that one should not give a child a name that is potentially embarrassing, degrading, or that will induce ridicule, parents seem to do it anyway. In some cases, a person's name has caused him or her so much trauma that the only thing that worked was their actually changing it. (The way we suggest a person go about changing his name is as follows: We tell them to write down all the qualities they want in themselves that would depict their highest ideals. Then they are to meditate on these qualities and pray for a name that will evoke these qualities.)

One of the things we have noticed in rebirthing is a situation where a person is named after a dead relative. In certain extreme cases, this person has actually become "more dead" to be like that relative in order to make the family happy! Especially in families where death is "worshipped" and where death is considered a higher place, or especially where there is the unfortunate religious belief that the only way you can be with God is to die. *The problem then, is that every single time this person's name is said, all circuits are "triggered" around family death karma.* This should definitely be avoided. . .if you want a child to be himself and be fully alive.

Sometimes parents are so determined to have a child of a certain sex that they only pick a name for that sex. God forbid if the child comes out a different sex than they had planned! In all of the years of our rebirthing work, we have seen a tremendous amount of confusion, hurt, and trauma in people who didn't come out the sex their parents wanted. Needless to say, parents must be careful to avoid the temptation of planning for and assuming they will have a child of a certain sex. Parents do not realize that they are not only making it hard on the child, but on themselves as well. If they want a boy, and the child is a girl, she may grow up trying to please them by becoming boyish. Resist the temptation to control or plan. Accept totally what is given.

We had a case where the mother decided if she had another child it might "keep the husband home" for a change. She told her husband "I'll name it after you" to make the whole thing more tantalizing. So, the child, a girl, was named after her father. This produced not only sex identity anxiety, but the thought, "They don't want me for me." She felt her conception was a manipulation.

One should also resist the temptation to impose a high, spiritual name on a child unless it feels absolutely right. In one such case, a child was named Lotus Sun, but when he was three years old asked that his name be changed to Leo. On the other hand, naming a child after someone "bad"—like Adolf—can cause the child to act "bad."

Nicknames can be especially subtle in their influence. One client was called "Slick" a lot and turned into a fairly slippery character. Another was nicknamed "Bounce" and became a bouncer. A third was "Dopey" and, you guessed it, grew up to have a drug problem.

We cannot stress enough the importance of carefully considering the implications of the name one is considering for a baby. People named after very successful public figures often seem to be more successful. People named after saints often seem to become holy and are frequently involved in spiritual work. However, naming a baby after someone great can be asking that child to live up to great expectations, which can, in turn, lead to great disappointment. Although we have not yet done any professional studies in this area, we have noticed these things over and over again in our work.

V

BIRTH & BUSINESS

BIRTH & BUSINESS

It might just be that business loses billions of dollars a year as a result of the collective unconscious birth trauma of their employees. In this book, we focus mostly on the effect of birth on personal relationships, which we believe to be substantial to say the least. How our unconscious birth scenarios influence our pursuit of money, as well as our business relationships, is a subject well worth considering.

First of all, money is the world's greatest symbol of survival, so any thoughts we have about struggling to survive from birth would cast a shadow on our struggle to make it at the job. For most of us, it was a struggle to get here in the first place. The journey through the birth canal was a tight squeeze, took too long, and the support we received often felt painful.

Just getting to work in the morning can be a re-creation of the birth scenario. Indeed, just waking up activates the subconscious memories. Every morning we wake up, we move from darkness to light, from quiet to noise, from unconsciousness to consciousness. The thoughts we have each morning, such as, "I don't want to get up," "I don't want to go to work," or, "I want to bury my head in the pillow," represent the primal emotions of birth.

If businesses knew what time of day their employees were born, they could orchestrate work schedules more effectively. Most people are born in the early morning. No wonder we create rush hours and traffic jams on our way to work. Rush hour is simply the collective birth trauma of thousands of people trying to make it at the same time. We even tend to create tunnels or bridges or "merging traffic" to indicate the tight squeeze through the birth canal. (In New York City, thousands of people get stuck in the Holland Tunnel each morning, which leads to none other than Canal Street!)

The boss often gets set up as the obstetrician. We have a strong desire to please him, gain his approval, make his job easier. For if we don't, he could cut the cord, that is, fire us. We may also project our hate for our obstetrician onto him and get even by not doing the job well!

The paycheck represents survival to most employees. It is their umbilical cord, their lifeline. The constant threat of separation from the job—which somehow represents mother to the subconscious mind—makes work even more fearful and a greater struggle. As businesses learn that "stress reduction" is just the beginning of what is needed, the possibility for increasing workers' efficiency by assisting them in releasing their primal panic becomes very real. Rebirthing might be thought of as "STRESS REDUCTION PLUS!" In other words, reducing stress is obviously significant; releasing the source of stress is the final solution! The purpose of all personal growth is, in a sense, to release all conflict, for once conflict is released, people tend to be more creative, productive, successful, and satisfied in their lives. And what is conflict if not the resistance to life itself? And this resistance is something we've carried with us since birth, which was such an unexpected intrusion on our blissful experience of life in the womb. We all want to re-experience that pervasive and harmonious sense of well-being we felt in the womb. But the memory of birth keeps rearing its suspicious head! Rebirthing could be for the American business what Tai-chi is to China or Zen to Japan—it could be our greatest natural resource yet untapped. And all it is is breath—air itself!

Since most people are used to the struggle they had in the birth canal, they tend to re-create this familiar struggle in order to "make it" in all areas of their lives.

Since most people needed an obstetrician in order to make it in the first place, they tend to believe they can't make it on their own and, therefore, set up obstetrician substitutes to be dependent on.

Depending on the particular circumstances of an individual's birth, different motivation techniques might prove to be more effective. For example, if someone was a "forceps birth," he will not respond well to pressure tactics; if someone was a "cesarian birth," he needs to be encouraged to find his own creative solutions; if someone was an "induced birth," he might be weak at decision-making. This is a whole new area of study, and we are mentioning it here in the hope that it will promote future in-depth studies on the subject. We would be interested to cooperate in these studies as rebirthers.

One thing is certain: birth was our first experience of labor and, as such, colors all our future experiences of going to work!

Businesses do lose billions of dollars annually as a result of employees who are either weak, helpless, and incompetent at the job, or those who act out their helplessness pattern by taking "sick leave" and collecting "disability." Much of what seems to be helplessness is actually the subconscious memory of birth surfacing with respect to work. Since work represents labor, and we all felt helpless about making it in the first place, we will tend to act this out in our relationship to the office. Offices even look like hospitals in their antiseptic aura.

It has been discovered, for example, that giving people "well days"—time off for good behavior—acts as preventative medicine for "sick days." It might also be true that giving employees an occasional "helpless day"—time to do nothing and be pampered—might further reduce the need for "sick days." The point here is that the more that businesses consciously participate in the well-being of their employees, the more their businesses will profit, financially and spiritually.

Another area worth investigating is the relationship between the "Personal Law" and the job. The personal law is our most negative belief about ourselves, a thought we concluded at birth as an explanation for our treatment. Some personal laws are: "I'm bad!"; "There's something wrong with me;" "I'm wrong;" "I can't make it;" "I'm a disappointment;" "I'm stupid." We tend to live our lives in overcompensation for our fear of the personal law being true.

For example, someone whose law is "I'm stupid" would overcompensate by being the smartest person in the class, at the job, etc. But since his smartness was based on his fear of being discovered as stupid, he would feel little safety and satisfaction in his intelligence. As an employee, he would live in dread of doing something stupid, which would motivate him to struggle harder to be smarter. His fear would often cause him to have occasional bouts of stupidity. If you are the employer of such a person, it would be wise to remember to acknowledge this person's intelligence regularly, remind him that he is bright, that you know it, and that he can relax into the knowledge of this, rather than struggle to prove it. This will cause immediate stress reduction, loss of struggle, and increased efficiency for your employee.

Similarly, if you have an employee whose law is, perhaps, "I'm a disappointment" (maybe her father wanted a boy, not a girl), it would be wise to know this and act accordingly. Someone who is afraid of being a disappointment could try hard to please you, customers, and co-workers, but often may actually create rejection on the job and act out being a disappointment. A good way to treat such a staff member would be to continuously reassure her that she is a wonderful surprise (the opposite of disappointment). You might actually use phrases like, "That's surprisingly good!" Or, "I'm surprised no one thought of that before," in praising this person. Acknowledgement works well in handling people with sensitive personal laws.

Again, this is an area that needs additional study. The relationship between prenatal psychology and business relationships is an infant science. But it is one that warrants further research, both from the financial and psychological points of view!

VI

COMPLETION:
A GREAT PLACE
TO START

COMPLETION: A GREAT PLACE TO START

Many people find they have trouble completing things. Be it an old relationship, a business project, a creative endeavor, a simple letter, they find themselves procrastinating, going unconscious, starting something new before they have finished something old.

Many potentially successful business plans are abandoned shortly before their culmination. Many potentially wonderful relationships are aborted when one or both of the partners cannot see the light at the end of the tunnel.

What is it about completion that makes it so difficult? Usually, the physical part of completing something is simple and straightforward. It's the emotional aspect that seems to paralyze people.

To complete is to let go of something old and start over again. In every completion is a little birth. We know artists who can't sell their paintings because they want to hold on to them as though they were their mother's breast. We know successful businessmen who could be more successful if they weren't so afraid to finish things faster and get on with new ideas. We know people who could have great relationships if they would only let go of the grief, pain, and mourning over a past lover.

It seems we are all addicted to the past. At least we know what it is. Maybe its very familiarity reminds us of the womb. Most people would rather hold on to something old, familiar, and imperfect than take the risk of letting it go to make room for something altogether new, unknown, and unfamiliar. Completion represents the cutting of the umbilical cord to our subconscious minds. As such, it tends to throw us into a primal panic.

These are affirmations we suggest you breathe into to reverse the condition of "completion trauma:"

(1) *It's fun to start over!*
(2) *It's safe to let go of the past.*
(3) *My future is safe and full of wonderful surprises.*
(4) *God has something better in store for me.*
(5) *I no longer need to hold on to survive.*
(6) *I already made it.*

Often we feel that incompletion keeps us alive—as long as we prolong the moment of delivery, we stay stuck in the process of struggling to make it, and it is this struggle that keeps us alive. Not so. You can survive without struggle.

(7) *It's easy for me to get what I want.*
(8) *I can make it easily and pleasurably.*
(9) *I no longer have to postpone completion in order to survive.*
(10) *The more I complete, the more alive I feel.*
(11) *It's a pleasure to complete things.*
(12) *It's fun to finish.*

We also tend to associate completion with death, which would inhibit anyone from finishing anything. The purpose of rebirthing is to lift you off the birth/death cycle so that you can experience life as a continuum, a series of here-and-nows, as opposed to an inevitable, linear march of beginnings, middles, and end.

(13) *My life urge is strengthened by completing things.*
(14) *I am rejuvenated by all my completions.*
(15) *Greater aliveness and success is inevitable for me.*
(16) *The more I complete things, the more I choose life.*
(17) *The more I choose life, the more I complete things.*
(18) *I am safe and immortal right now!*

VII

APPENDIX

OTHER UNUSUAL TYPES
OF RELATIONSHIPS

More research needs to be done on other types of birth that are unusual, such as:

> Babies born with the amniotic sac intact
> Babies born with birth defects
> Babies born with an arm presentation
> Babies born with RH factor/Toxemia/Blue Babies
> Triplets and Quads
> Babies born from implantations and modern methods of fertilization

We have also had interesting cases (not yet written up) of people born during major disasters or catastrophes, such as:

> Babies born in war zones, especially bombings during wars
> Babies born the day a president was assassinated
> Babies born during hurricanes, tornadoes, earthquakes etc.
> Babies born during other surprising catastrophes

And then there are babies born in surprising ways, in undesirable spaces, such as:

> Babies born in taxi cabs
> Babies born in elevators

It makes one wonder, doesn't it, how these factors affect our relationships!

BIRTH TRAUMA & TEEN SUICIDE

In 1986, *USA Today* reported the findings of research conducted by Lee Salk at the Cornell University Medical College in New York. Originally reported in the British medical journal *Lancet*, the study found that teenagers who commit suicide are more likely to have suffered health problems at birth—or had mothers who were sick during their pregnancy.

The researchers cautioned that the link between prebirth or at-birth problems and subsequent suicide in later years is not necessarily a direct one, but that there seems to be an increased risk for teenagers who had suffered such problems at birth.

Salk was quoted as saying: "What it suggests is that kids who have problems at birth or even before are more vulnerable to the stresses of life later on, to the point of taking their own life."

Salk studied 156 teenagers. Fifty-two of them committed suicide and 104 had not. Teen suicides have increased some 300% in the last 30 years, and Salk noticed that there had been no increase in the overall rate of suicide in the general population during the same period. Salk sought to understand what factors might play a role in this 300% increase *only* among teenagers, while the general population did not experience the same rate. Increased stress and social problems obviously would not account for such a skyrocketing rate in only one social group.

Salk discovered the following factors were among those factors that might play a role in teenage suicide: mothers who suffered chronic disease during pregnancy (including anemia, arthritis, hypertension, asthma, hepatitis, and obesity; respiratory distress experienced by the baby in the early hours following birth; mothers who had inadequate prenatal care during their first 20 weeks of pregnancy.

A FEW WORDS ON REBIRTHING

by Bob Mandell

It is our experience that most people who are exposed to birth information such as you have received here, are ripe for the process of rebirthing. Often, just reading about birth-related experiences can stimulate unconscious memories, feelings and body sensations from your own birth.

If you feel a little out of your body, spacey, disoriented, frustrated or confused, we sincerely suggest that you consider the possibility that you are experiencing a spontaneous rebirth. Such occurrences are common, but usually unidentified as such. Some of you might feel inspired to pursue the rebirthing process as a result of connections you have made between your birth and relationships from reading this book.

Rebirthing is a truly unique and wonderful experience. It's a way to bring all personal growth home to your mind, body and spirit. It is an extremely sensitive and personal process that you should do only in the best of all possible circumstances. It's worth searching for the right rebirther for you.

There are many excellent rebirthers throughout the world. The Loving Relationships Training, which we conduct, only sponsors those rebirthers we consider to be fully trained to guide people through this remarkable experience, people who have experienced and healed the effects of their own births on their relationships, family and the world. To be acknowledged as an LRT (Loving Relationships Training) sponsored rebirther, one must not only be adept at the breathing process that is the essence of rebirthing; one must also have come to peace in one's relationships, vis-a-vis one's mother and father, siblings, etc. The reason for this is that we believe that the consequences of birth on relationships, and the consequences of family on your personal growth are equally powerful forces which cannot be ignored on the journey to more loving, free and spontaneous relationships. Rebirthing is ultimately a whole healing tool, which, when experienced in the presence of a guide who knows the full ramifications of birth on relationships, can be an extraordinary awakening and release into more unconditionally loving relationships.

For further information on rebirthing, the Loving Relationships Training, and sponsored rebirthers closest to you, please call:

LRT International
1-800-INTL-LRT
or
212-799-7323

Sondra Ray and Bob Mandel have created a number of cassette tapes designed to support people in healing the effects of the past on current relationships. For information regarding any of these tapes, which include:

> Your Ideal Relationship
> Sex and Relationships
> Having It All
> Amazing You
> Peace With Passion
> Money Montras

contact the LRT International Office, 145 W. 87th Street, New York, New York 10024, or call

1-800-INTL-LRT
or
212-799-7323

A WORD FROM THE PUBLISHER

Celestial Arts is the publisher of many excellent books on personal growth, health, and wellness, with an emphasis on topics of awareness such as rebirthing, meditation, consciousness, and miracles.

Among our bestselling authors is Sondra Ray—founder of the *Loving Relationships Training* and author of *Drinking the Divine, I Deserve Love, Celebration of Breath, The Only Diet There Is, Ideal Birth,* and *Rebirthing in the New Age*.

We also publish Virginia Satir, Richard Moss, Barry Stevens, Jerry Jampolsky, Kenneth R. Pelletier, Alan Watts, Emmett E. Miller, and Elson M. Haas.

We also publish children's books and a complete line of posters and graphics.

For a copy of our free catalog, write or call: Celestial Arts, P.O. Box 7327, Berkeley, CA 94707 (415) 524-1801.

A WORD FROM TEN SPEED PRESS

In 1983 *Celestial Arts* became a part of *Ten Speed Press,* publishers of career and life guidance books including *What Color Is Your Parachute?,* and other books on bicycling, outdoors, and cookbooks. Please write or call for their free catalog: Ten Speed Press, P.O. Box 7123, Berkeley, CA 94707 (415) 845-8414.